An Old Breviary

TYTINILLUS *(See page 84)*

Autobiography of an Old Breviary

Edited By REV. HERMAN J. HEUSER, D.D.

MEDIATRIX PRESS
MMXXII

ISBN: 9781957066134

Nihil Obstat.
ARTHUR J. SCANLAN, S. T. D.
Censor Librorum.

Imprimatur.
PATRICK, CARDINAL HAYES
Archbishop of New York, *New York, March* 22, 1925

©Mediatrix Press.
All rights reserved. With the exception of short excerpts used in critical review no part of this work may be reproduced in physical or electronic format without the express permission of the publisher. No part of this edition may be placed on archive.org.

An Autobiography of an Old Breviary, originally published by Benziger Brothers 1925, is in the public domain. Editorial changes and typography are the property of Mediatrix Press.

Mediatrix Press
607 E 6th Ave.
Post Falls, ID 83854
www.mediatrixpress.com

CONTENTS

First Part

I. How the totum came to tell its story 5
II. The breviary goes on an ocean voyage 9
III. The padre discourses with a minister's wife and an American judge 14
IV. The judge investigates the insides of the totum. He is interrupted by a question about irish manuscripts 23
V. The totum gives a tip to the preacher 36
VI. The breviary in the police station 38
VII. A ride in the pullman car. 41
VIII. A chat with sophia 46
IX. Arrival, on terra firma. The totum pays a visit to a convent of nuns. 48
X. A talk with the abbess. The padre asks the advice of the totum 51
XI. What happens in the chapel, and in the "enclosed garden" of our lady. 56

Second Part

I. The Totum Gets an American Orderly 65
II. A Point of Regularity in the Life of the Totum . . . 68
III. The Padre Studies the Calendar 69
IV. How Pope Gregory the Great Fixed the Sun-dial   72
V. The Golden Number, and What Comes of It 73

Third Part

I. At Home and in the Seminary 79
II. The Padre Takes the Totum to School 82
III. He Draws a Picture of Titynillus and His Wicked

Ways 84
IV. The Traveling Cleric 87
V. The Padre Becomes Critical. 88

Fourth Part

I. The Noble Pedigree of the Totum 93
II. The Ordinary of the Office 99
III. The Invitatory 101
IV. Intoning the Antiphons 104
V. The Ninety-fourth Psalm 105
VI. Cardinal Quiñones and His Breviary 110
VII. Talks about Reforming the Totum 113

Fifth Part

I. The Seven Hours of the Divine Office 117
II. The Roman and the Gallican Psalter 122
III. The Second Nocturn. 125
IV. The Gregorian Method to Be Upset 128
V. "Confitemini Domino". 130
VI. "Beatus Vir". 136
VII. The Bishop Examines 142
VIII. The Golden Alphabet. 146

Sixth Part

I. The Totum Gets a Vacation 153
II. New Life and Hebrew Music 156
III. Deacon Tim Wants to Know More about the
    Christian Poets 165
IV. The Last "Drop" and the Totum Is Pensioned. . . 178

GLOSSARY 181
INDEX 191

Introduction

HE story of an old Breviary is here introduced with a view of interpreting, in a familiar way, the object, nature, and contents of the official prayer-book of the Catholic Church.

Shortly after the first part of it had appeared in the *Ecclesiastical Review* the editor was requested to have the introductory chapter printed in pamphlet, since it was thought that so it might serve the apologetic purpose of explaining to laymen, even to those outside the Catholic fold, the magnificent philosophy of continuous worship as practiced in the Roman Catholic Church. The secret of the union that binds habitually together the members of the Catholic priesthood, in a common language, all over the world, despite the differences of education, nationality and race, is found in the virtue of a common prayer such as the unique form of the Roman Breviary represents. But as we had intended to give the story, as far as practicable, in continuous series, for the benefit of the clerical readers of the *Review,* after which it might appear in book form, we could not well enter upon the project of a partial publication.

On consulting the publishers of the prospective volume their advice caused us to alter the original project, and to discontinue the serial, for the purpose of issuing the whole at once in a volume which would allow the reader to keep in mind the connection of such parts as intimately bear upon each other, and that serve as mutual illustration of the different elements which make up the structure of the Canonical Office.

In its present form the story is intended, in the first place, for priests who want to get a fuller appreciation of

INTRODUCTION

the beauty and grace of their daily office of prayer than they may have received from the didactic lessons in the liturgy class of the Seminary course.

In the next place, it is meant for students in theology, who are preparing for Sacred Orders, and who need to know the structure, use, and purpose of the prayer which, in the deeper appreciation of its admirable form, offers them the true motives of personal sanctification, while at the same time it opens the manifold channels of grace which the united devotion, every day, offers to the faithful at the hands and from the hearts of their shepherds throughout Christendom.

Finally, it may aid numerous souls who in the retirement of the cloister seek to sanctify their daily labors by the thoughtful recitation of the Canonical Hours.

While the lessons which the story is intended to impart, are more or less concealed amidst the incidents of daily experience in a priestly life, they review the more important elements which make up the grace-imparting collection of prayers, readings and liturgical illustrations of the Divine Office. For the convenience of those who read the Roman Breviary in English, some unfamiliar terms are briefly explained in a *Glossary* at the end of the volume.

THE EDITOR.

Autobiography of an Old Breviary

First Part

I. How the Totum Came to Tell Its Story

I AM put on the shelf. The sexton of St. Bridget's had fetched me from the hospital called the "Bindery," where I had been under repairs after an accident. But when Father Tim saw me, he didn't like the looks of my new overcoat. He said I was a "Totum" and a bit heavy anyhow; and, though we had been chums ever since his ordination way back twenty years ago, a new edition, a lightweight from some place in Germany, where they know how to make books, caught his fancy because it was dressed in Russian leather.

Now I am too old to be jealous, but the thought of being accounted toothless after long and faithful service rankles, and I am resolved to leave the record of it, and of my experiences among the clerical brethren, for posterity. Father Tim is a Limerick man, but his bishop sent him to Innsbruck, to the Jesuits, to study, and I am afraid that has made him partial to the Germans. However, he is a good sort and when he and his neighbor, Father O'More, go on their annual fishing trip for vacation in the early summer, they have rare fun. Hereafter I shall not be with them, I know, and indeed, the fishing trip is the cause of my being exiled to solitary contemplation. It happened this way.

Father Tim and his chum, when on their trout-trolling holiday, are in the habit of lodging at the house of a prosperous farmer. They have the second-story front—two rooms with a porch to look down from. One sultry afternoon when the twain had returned earlier than usual, Father Tim took me out on the porch for an airing and his orison. Just in the middle of the second nocturn, where it tells how St. Juliana *"in stomachi morbum incidit,"* there was a tremendous racket below. A stray heifer had gone into the yard and awakened opposition of a proprietary nature in a young collie on the ground. Now Father Tim was what his people called "a pious priest." Father O'More was not. He was a bit "practical," and sometimes provoked mild remonstrance from his companion for the way he would invoke "Holy Moses." On this occasion it was Father O'More who tried to manage the campaign, for the dog was his, with the result that the heifer upset a beehive, which invited impolite comment on the part of the priest, to the horror of his clerical brother above. Father Tim, trying to locate the scene of havoc and battle, craned his neck to the side of the house, and in doing so unwittingly dropped me over the railing that guarded the porch.

The fall broke my back. They gathered me up tenderly, but the damage was done, and the *Pars Æstiva* had to be amputated then and there. That evening began the alienation of my affections. Father Tim borrowed a dudish breviary from his confrère, and in doing so made sundry disparaging remarks about my age, and my being heavy and superannuated. It was little consolation to hear that he would have me mended, as I was a keepsake, a gift from a venerable seminary professor, and all that sort of thing. That didn't mollify me a bit, especially as I was subjected to all kinds of cutting remarks and poundings by an ill-mannered doctor whose name was "Binder" and who had no regard for old age.

Nor have I fared much better since I came back to the parochial home. It is evident that my old master is satisfied to put me on the retired list, superannuated. He said they had made new laws in Rome, and—well I had better keep quiet about that, for of course I am a Roman. But now, since there is leisure for reflection about my past career, I recall that there is a streak of the Gallican in me. My remote ancestors bore the name of *Mizmor*,[1] which sounds like Hebrew, and perhaps my forbears were from one of the lost tribes that came over to Gaul and to Ireland. (Anyhow *Mizmor* sounds Irish like "Lismore.") Then they were converted by St. Jerome and intermarried with Greek emigrants from Egypt and adopted the name *Psalterium*. Eventually they came under Roman dominion, and so I am a true Roman. With intermarriages the name changed and eventually became *Breviary*, with the surname *Totum*. And so here I am a Roman Totum Breviary.

As *Totum* I saw the light first in Belgium. My baptismal certificate dates from Tournai (Tornaci Nerviorum). My godfather was a bishop. The first impression that has remained with me through life after leaving the nursery in the parental home—the incunabula—is that of a school conducted by Desclée and Lefevre, under the tutorship of the fellows of St. John's. When we were released from their discipline we accounted ourselves well-read *(rubricated* was the college term), and a great prelate who belonged to the Index Congregation, and who examined us according to the text-books, page by page, certified by diploma that we had on the whole made an excellent impression, and that we were really typical products of a great university, such as the Catholic Church.

We were of course bound to observe regulation

---

[1] Hebrew for *Psalm*.

form—black; which meant that we must stick to our colors. Next we received introductions and recommendations, gilt-edged certificates. Our titles, to indicate affiliations, were duly impressed upon us. Some of us also had our ribbons of distinction. Thus equipped we were ready for active service, and only awaited the proper call. Meanwhile we went into retreat. Since we were to devote ourselves to prayer and spiritual instruction we began to ascend the higher flights of the upper storerooms. Swathed in somber brown we passed several weeks in close retirement, with hardly a sound to disturb our repose away from the world of traffic.

    Then one morning there came an order to send down "par ascenseur" a dozen sets of the Desclée Breviaires. We were all of us to be shipped by freight express to the Grand Seminaire at Malines. Here an officious cleric placed us in line for the inspection of some ecclesiastical dignitary. With the latter was a bespectacled elderly abbé who at once unceremoniously laid hold on me, and peering sharply, looked right through me. Although I was a bit disconcerted and not disposed to be very confidential to a perfect stranger, I thought it best to be open and began to show forth my perfections at the "Commune Sanctorum," when he promptly shut me up, and simply uttered "Bien!", tucked me under his left arm and marched me off. I felt rather constrained and wondered what might become of me, but in a little while we were respectfully accosted by a young seminarist who inquired at what time "Monsieur l'abbé" was to leave for Brussels. Elated, I began to—but now came a revelation. We were going to America. My new godfather was the rector of a Western seminary in the United States. Hurrah! I would begin my *carriera* by travel abroad, not as an adjunct to mere missionary rectors and assistants such as commonly went to the States—no, as the intimate adviser and confidential companion of a learned academician, a possible monsignor, perhaps a future bishop who would caress me with a beringed hand, and permit me to live near a pectoral cross, the awe-inspired envy of common folk who could boast of no familiarity with mitered heads. Think of it! He would carry me in processions and on visitations. I nearly jumped out of this reverend rector's tight hold of me with the joy of it all.

II. The Breviary Goes on an Ocean Voyage

How we got to Southampton I do not know, for somehow the professor had overlooked my importance and locked me in his valise with some rather disreputable associates, among whom I recall a pair of boots, a hairbrush, a box of Roman collars, and a cigar case. But on the vessel I was released from the unsavory companionship and restored to my proper dignity when, in the evening—it was Saturday—the abbé took me into the dining salon to read Matins and Lauds for the following day.

While we were thus engaged in respectful intercourse, a lady approached and inquired whether there would be divine service on the morrow. As we had not had an opportunity to ascertain whether there were any Catholics among the few passengers of the ship, my master answered somewhat hesitatingly that he didn't know, but that the captain would no doubt make the customary announcement, that evening.

"Are you not a minister of the Gospel?" she inquired.

"I am a priest," was the reply.

"Oh—I thought you were reading the Bible—and so I

spoke to you. Pardon me for intruding."

"You are quite right, madam," said the priest. "What I am reading is the Bible."

"But Catholics do not pay much heed to Bible reading," she rejoined. "Your dogma is, if I understand rightly, the Church."

"Yes, the Church, which the Bible teaches us to obey, bids Catholics read it continually in one part or another of her daily public service. Besides that, we priests bind ourselves at our ordination by vow to spend each day at least an hour or more in the reading of the Bible." So saying, he handed me to her.

"You see, if you note the place where the marker is inserted, the day and even the hour assigned for the reading, which is not optional but definitely prescribed."

She took me with somewhat shy curiosity and looked into my face:

"Oh, but it is Latin!"

"Yes, the language of our early Christian forefathers and religious teachers. It preserves unchanged the apostolic traditions in a classical tongue of the past that has not been tampered with."

"But are Catholics sufficiently familiar with the dead language to make it the expression of their hearts and to enter into the sense of the inspired words?"

"It is the chief business of those who are priests to interpret the original text according to the ancient traditions. These traditional interpretations are found here side by side with the text of the Bible. As for the priests knowing the Latin, they have hardly much choice, seeing that their training in the seminary covers as a rule a ten-year course during which the Latin language is the ordinary object and vehicle of instruction in at least the theological and philosophical disciplines."

THE BREVIARY ON A VOYAGE 11

"But do they teach the people this same knowledge?"

"They could hardly do otherwise, if they teach at all, considering that the matter is of obligation and can easily be verified by those who happen to know Latin."

"That sounds marvelous," she replied with her look fixed on me. "I do not know Latin and cannot read this. But I do not doubt the truth of what you say. I am just returning from Australia, where my husband has been engaged as a missionary for some years. I am sure neither of us is aware that your Church is particularly partial to the Bible."

Later on, the conversation was resumed among a number of passengers who had met at the captain's table and to whom the lady had mentioned her astonishing discovery. She had evidently told them about the priest aboard who read the Bible every day, and what he had said about Catholics reading it habitually. Since I was the object of the discussion I felt my importance considerably increased and made every effort to be on my good behavior.

The incident set me reflecting, and the result of my meditations I shall here summarize before relating my further experiences during more than a quarter of a century of service. I was aware that I was the official prayer-book of the clergy, and that my relatives were all on familiar terms with ecclesiastical dignitaries of every degree, even hobnobbing with the Pope and the Cardinals. But I had never realized, until I heard the professor, that I was actually inspired and ranked with the Sacred Scriptures. The Abbé Hogan, as they called my master, explained it all very simply to a little group of interested passengers, among whom were a few Catholics who hardly seemed conscious that they had ever read the Bible. Later on, he brought me into the liturgy class of the theological seminary. Then I began to know something about my insides, which I had never thought of. He laid bare the whole anatomy, brain and heart, and liver and lungs. But I shall come to that when we get to America.

Meanwhile he dwelt on the fact that I—the Breviary—was simply an organism which represented a systematic course in devotional Bible-reading and its interpretation. Each day a portion of the Psalter is recited so as to cover the hundred and fifty Psalms within the week. The other sections of the Bible are so apportioned that the whole series of historical, sapiential, and prophetic books is read within the course of a year. The Gospels and a number of the Epistles from the New Testament are read on the fifty-two Sundays of the year at the obligatory service of the Mass, and some of them are reserved for special festivals of the liturgical cycle.

But not only is the whole Bible thus practically covered in Catholic public worship within the course of the year, it is also commented upon and explained so as to serve the priest for meditation, and to furnish him with authoritative teaching for the people. Thus I am really a model of the safest kind to learn from, a perfect organism and thoroughly sound in every part, except perhaps in the uninspired illustrations from the "Proprium Sanctorum." But even there you cannot pick many flaws, since I always maintain the principle of edification. Of this more anon, when I come to make confession of my casual imperfections. Just now I am concerned with explaining my last end and purpose of creation, together with the leading traits of my character—honestly.

The chief characteristic of our family is indicated by my ancestral name, which still is kept in the baptismal register of every new offspring as it is brought to the

Church. I mean the *Psalter*. The Psalms are part of my daily offering, because they are prayers as well as subjects of meditation. But the rest of the Sacred Books are also incorporated in me, so that through the Hebrew origin of my ancestry I am related to Moses, the Prophets, and even the New Testament writers. You will recognize the characteristics and moods of the inspired authors in me at certain seasons of the year as follows:

In *Advent* I announce the coming of Christ by the prophecies of *Isaiah*.

During *Christmastide* I enlarge upon the benefits of Christ's coming in the reading of the *Epistles of St. Paul* to the Romans, Corinthians, Galatians, Ephesians, Philippians, Colossians, and Thessalonians. Then in his letters to Timothy, Titus, Philemon, and lastly to the Hebrews.

With *Lent* (beginning at Septuagesima) I inculcate the principles and observance of law by the reading of the five *Books of Moses*—the creation of the world; man's fall; the restoration through the teaching of the Law; and the promise of new grace in the Messianic Redemption.

Then follows *Passiontide*, with the call to penance by the Prophet *Jeremias* as a condition of salvation and participation in the Redemption.

The *Easter* cycle brings with it the reading of the first period of the history of the Church, the thirty years of apostolic upbuilding on the foundations of Christ, the Cornerstone, in the *Acts of the Apostles*. This is followed by the description of the heavenly Jerusalem, the Church perfected, in the story of the *Apocalypse*.

Next comes the feast of *Pentecost*, with its expansions of the work of the Paraclete on earth, the gradual record of which finds its prophetic counterpart in the history of Samuel the High Priest as related in the *Books of Kings*.

The few months that follow are filled with instructions represented in the didactic and prophetic books, containing practical lessons of right living and warnings. They are divided so as to give readings for

August: *Proverbs, Ecclesiastes, Wisdom, Ecclesiasticus;*[2]
September: *Job, Tobias, Judith, Esther;*
October: *Two Books of the Maccabees;*
November: *Ezechiel, Daniel* and the Minor Prophets.

The books of the Bible are thus woven into a continuous scheme for devotional and instructive reading. They make up in the Totum a harmonious pattern of liturgical worship by the insertion of appropriate prayer, canticle, and reflection. At one time they were published under the titles of Psalters and Lectionaries. But my godfather made it understood that our race developed and that in me—the *Totum Breviarium Romanum*—you have a fine specimen of the whole Bible properly annotated. He indicated that I am of aristocratic descent and in every way worthy to be treated with respect and thoughtful attention.

III. The Padre Discourses with a Minister's Wife and an American Judge

The professor was sick (mal-de-mer), and stayed in his berth this morning. Sunday, hm! and we were to have a long chat together, with "Confitemini" and the Athanasian Creed in it. Our room-mate, a dapper, middle-aged man, dentist by profession, asked:

"Dominie, can I do anything for you?"

He got only a groaned "No, thank you, Doctor," for

---

[2] Sirach in modern Bibles.

A MINISTER'S WIFE AND A JUDGE

answer and went out.

Now I know the Padre was thinking of me. It had become evident in the few days of our acquaintance with each other that he was a regular man. Every morning, thus far, he had said his Little Hours before breakfast. Today he had omitted both Hours and breakfast, and it was already past the time, for the luncheon gong had sounded twice. When the steward came to inquire whether the professor wanted anything, and suggested a cup of coffee as being both a sedative and stimulant, the patient consented with an air of mild disgust.

Meanwhile I was lying on the ledge of the washstand, a most undignified position for one of my ancestry and connections. But I have learnt to keep shut up when not specially wanted or not in proper company. I knew the professor could not get along without me for any length of time, and so I waited quietly. During the few days which I spent in the Malines Seminary, I had seen a young tonsured cleric lift up one of my relations from the top of a dust-bin where it had been carelessly laid and, after touching it with his lips, put it reverently on the prie-dieu. So I knew that my family was to be respected. But I was not disturbed until the late afternoon, when the weather cleared, and the doctor had said the professor would be better on deck.

So we went up, my master and I, to sit in a sheltered seat on the lee side of the boat. We were silent, although I was there on his lap ready to open the conversation. He was in a devout mood, too, as I suspect people generally are when seasick; but the flesh is weaker than the spirit. I am glad I have no flesh, only spirit. Well, there we both lay without a word, the neighbors smiling on us benevolently and making an occasional attempt at encouragement or greeting. After a short hour someone invited the Padre to go in and take a tonic; it was in the days when champagne was thought good for the seasick. Since then the philosophy of life has changed and there is a mileage limit which bars the spirit. It is pleasant to carry one's spirit within oneself, as I do, and it suffices for all emergencies, though the Father does not seem to think so. Well, he went in under benevolent escort and left me covered with a rug on the deck-chair.

After a while I heard low sounds of talking among the passengers of the adjoining row of seats. They were interested in the Padre. It was clear from what they said that they were observing him closely, though accusingly estranged from him.

"Who is he?"

"Oh, an American priest, professor somewhere in a Western college."

"I heard Mr. Morris, the lawyer, say he was a Belgian, a well-informed man, and nice spoken. He had several conversations with him."

"I am afraid of these priests," said a woman who was knitting. "I wonder if they are sincere or what they ordinarily seem to be. One hears so much about Jesuits and their duplicity."

"Well, I think priests are the least mysterious beings under the sun. Why, you can see their good-nature oozing out of every feature —their jolly faces, words, the way their own people 'Father' them. One can hardly imagine them to be anything else but good-natured. Now and then you meet the sober, ascetical kind, like this professor; but there is never anything to suggest the sanctimonious or hypocritical in them.

"All the same, you have history—Richelieu, Mazarin, and the Inquisition, to show that the priesthood is ambitious and, when in power, cruel. I was in Spain and saw enough of the marks of clerical persecution to make one shudder at the sight of a monk."

"What did you see!"

"Why I saw the very instruments they used in torturing the heretics and Jews—thumbscrews, stocks, chains, and other devices of torture; it was awful"

"Did you see priests using them on the heretics and Jews?"

"No, but—"

"But history, as we usually read it, is to be trusted as much for veracity, just as much, as your political column of the party newspaper. No doubt there was fanaticism and there was even malice among ecclesiastics in power during the Middle Ages, as there is at all times; but just as historians call by the name 'Dark Ages' the period when the magnificent works of architectural art were produced through the industry of the guilds, which were dominated by religious motives, so we label with 'Inquisition' the ages when the scriptoria of the monks preserved for us the copies of the Bible and the grand works of literature by which alone the principles of charity and a high standard of public morality were and are maintained in what we call Christian civilization. The institutions of philanthropy and learning which freed the slave, combated Turkish rapacity, established the great universities of Paris, Oxford, Padua, are the outcome of what you call the 'Dark Ages' and monastic ignorance. Without them what would our modern literature and laboratories be? No, I am not a Catholic, but I see the historic Church and its institutions, of which the priesthood is an essential part, in a very different light."

How I chuckled when he mentioned the Bible and the scriptoria of the monks. I almost jumped off the deck-chair, but managed to hold my covers shut fast, despite the breeze around me.

The minister's wife, mentioned in the early part of my story, spoke up also. She had thought the clergyman was a very respectable gentleman and had explained the use of the priests' prayer-book in a way that surprised her, and yet she could not doubt that he spoke the truth. "Of course, the exclusiveness with which Romans look upon their Church is somewhat bewildering and savors of narrow bigotry."

"Why should it? If truth is to be found through the Bible, that book must have a uniform interpretation which excludes all contradiction or variety. Christ wanted His followers to be one, united in charity. Protestantism represents anything but unity and charity. Its philanthropic work is no more than that which you might expect from such pagan advocates as Marcus Aurelius, or Epictetus; whereas in the Catholic Church, whatever the abuses in individual cases, even among the clergy high up, including bishops and popes, you have doctrinal and disciplinary union. The standard of morals is always high if you go to the sources of its teaching and the reform legislation which stands for authority. I never see those Catholic nuns in their quests abroad, or at work in the hospitals, without feeling that they are wonderfully pure and self-sacrificing. The Catholic Church alone is responsible for such women by the thousands, in every land and under every condition—and the fact that they are not advertised, and indeed shun personal appraisal, unlike the Nightingales and stage heroines of philanthropy, is an argument in favor of the Catholic system."

A steward came out to fetch me and the robe. Well, I was pleased, for at bottom I came into a good deal of praise from the last speaker, who I learnt later was a New

A MINISTER'S WIFE AND A JUDGE

England judge, with a fine record in public life. In the next few days I saw much of him, for he took to the Father, and asked him about me, as I shall personally record with proper humility, since what was said is all true. And the minister's wife and some of the other first-class passengers listened with no little satisfaction to my apologist. But that was when the mal-de-mer had entirely gone, and we were sailing smoothly toward the Newfoundland coast.

"Mrs. Stafford, the Australian minister's wife, has been telling us about your Bible reading, Father. I see you keep it up. The matter suggests novel views, for we all share, I daresay, more or less the notion that Catholics are not as partial to the Bible as are Protestants." So spoke the Judge.

"Naturally—since the Bible furnishes the supreme and sole rule of faith to Protestants, who furthermore believe that that faith is the only guarantee of salvation."

"Well, do you not hold the same rule, inasmuch as the very existence and the doctrine of your Church rest, in the first place, on the statements of the Bible, which you maintain to be inspired. In fact, it seems true that you are guilty of what we lawyers call the argument of a vicious circle. You prove the truth of the Church from the Bible, and when asked for proof of the truth of the Bible, you appeal to the Church."

"Quite so. Only that a lawyer's distinction also happens to save us from what you call the 'vicious circle.' We believe the Bible to be divinely inspired and as such infallible, and we do so because the Church founded by Christ so teaches unequivocally. But our acceptance of the authority of the Church is based on an historical fact. You, as a lawyer, accept as evidence in any disputed case the truth of statements by witnesses whose veracity is attested by their conduct, and who are in position to vouch for the facts which they solemnly affirm. The Gospels, besides being religious books, are also historical documents. There are three of them by different writers, all of whom relate in substance the same facts, in very simple language not easily misunderstood. Whatever differences there are in the interpretation of doctrinal details, they all clearly state that there was such a person as Christ; that He claimed a Divine mission, and in fact died for that assertion; that He did very extraordinary things, such as curing diseases, multiplying bread, raising the dead, and rising from the grave as He had foretold; that in His claims to Divinity there was apparently no motive of ambition, no suspicion of fanaticism. On the contrary, His teaching has been recognized as a most wholesome, sober, and enduring philosophy, making for peace, unity, and contentment. Least of all have His sincerity and veracity been questioned or discredited after twenty centuries of strife in which every other philosophy of life has been tested.

"This person, Christ, claiming, teaching and demonstrating His power to perpetuate the principles of truth and justice for the good of mankind, stated that He meant to found a Church, a society in which these principles would be maintained through doctrine and discipline to the end of time, by the same Divine power that sent Him to announce the Gospel.

"Catholics claim that their Church is this society, and that its essential prerogatives are those claimed by its Founder—namely infallibility in teaching truth, and the gifts of healing the wounds, moral and physical, from which mankind suffers, just as Christ did for the generation in which He lived as man.

"So you see we accept the Bible as infallible, inspired

truth, because the Church teaches this fact. But the authority of the Church itself is not proved from the Bible, as an inspired book, but from such documentary evidence of history as men accept in everyday life."

Quite a group of listeners had gathered around us, and I felt very proud of the Padre when the Judge said—

"You are making a good case, and I have often in reading history thought that, if there is any creed that has a claim to consistent and reasonable existence it is the Roman Church. Its constitution and hierarchical government are, so far as I understand, very much like the Constitution and government of the United States. You have your pope chosen president by an electoral college made up of representatives from all classes and nationalities. Each diocese is, like our separate States, an independent administrative corporation, subject to the federal law of the Holy See, but otherwise independent."

"Quite so," said the Padre. "Each bishop is pope in his own diocese, and the diocesan laws or statutes are made by a synod. The bishop is guardian and responsible for his administration to the Roman Pontiff alone."

"I see. Probably that is the reason why the Roman Church has outlived all other governments. There are some things in your Church, however, which don't appeal to the outsider. One of them is the claim to temporal power and the interference of ecclesiastics in political — I mean international — affairs. Christ said, I believe, that His Kingdom was not of this world. He gave to Caesar the things that belong to Caesar. But the Church of Rome has its ambassadors, nuncios, and legates everywhere. Why not mind their religious business and teach goodness and obedience to civil law, and let the State attend to secular affairs?"

"For the simple reason," promptly answered the

Padre, "that a society which maintains both religious and secular interests is unable entirely to separate the two. You sentence a man to prison, Judge, because he has stolen, and the law says: 'Thou mayest not steal with impunity.' You punish him, but you do not necessarily correct him. Religion says, 'Thou shalt not steal,' and inculcates motives that not only correct the tendency or will to steal, but prevent it. The two authorities meet in the result, and unless they combine and have a mutual understanding to cooperate with each other, they will clash as inimical, just as the confirmed thief bent on stealing will hate and clash with the moral teacher who advocates honest methods.

"Temporal power in the Church means known freedom from the interference by such Secular powers as may prevent the free inculcation of motives which make its civil subjects obedient in principle to all just law, but hostile to rapacity, personal ambition, national pride, and emotional reform movements. There is no check to stay power, unless it recognizes Divine authority, and that authority must have the character and form of a religious organism. It cannot be made dependent on individual notions, even of irreproachable rulers, of what is right or wrong."

The call for dinner put an end to the conversation, and I felt that we—the Padre and I— had done good work for the day. I was left in the stateroom to reflect on my glorious prerogative of being the power behind the throne of the Padre; for, after all, as he had said, the institution of the Church by Christ is proved from the Bible, and that is myself—with comments, and goodly prayers and blessings. But the Padre has put me under his pillow, so it behooves us both to go to sleep.

IV. The Judge Investigates the Insides of the Totum. He Is Interrupted by a Question about Irish Manuscripts

The Padre and I spent most of the forenoon in the smoking-room. Fog, then rain, and sudden gusts of wind drove the passengers who did not stay in their bunks, to bundle themselves up in some corner, drowsing, reading, or playing solitaire. A steward was answering calls for "Rye," or "Scotch," or "Schiedam," which I thought very vulgar and profane; but the Judge was standing there at the bar—which I suppose was his proper position when there was no regular court in session—seeming to approve, since he liberally patronized the caviar sandwiches on the sideboard. I know now that it was all right, for there was no three-mile limit in those days to disturb the conscience of the smoking-room patrons. Anyhow, the Padre did not indicate any displeasure, from which I gathered that everything was proper, and that the occasional unsteadiness of gait was due merely to the restlessness of the sea and the rocking of the ship.

Now, the only one with whom my chief had thus far conversed this morning was myself. We had had an official talk, and the "Hours" had slipped by in what seemed less than fifteen minutes. But he had a way of quizzing me, studying my "insides," as Jinks would have said. I had heard him too announce at Louvain that he had to give a course of lectures in the fall to the second-year theologians on the "Anatomy of the Breviary." So he often handled me by way, presumably, of preparation, to get at my heart, noting in his little book the red lines—the arteries—under the name of Rubrics. A young man who had sat beside us made several attempts to engage the

Padre in conversation, but as he seemed rather too anxious to advertise some scheme for ventilating churches for which he must have been an agent, we took no particular interest in him. After a while he went away. Then the Judge came over and sat in his place.

"When the half-gods go, the gods arrive," he said. "Did that Jew get after you with his ventilators? Why, we have better ones in America. There, is nothing to be learnt by us from the Britisher,"

"Except it be respect for law, Judge," chimed in a sad-looking individual on the opposite side of the table. "What impressed me while over there was the way the English talk about their Queen and Ministers and House of Commons. They have government all right, and that's more than we can say over in the States, though I guess we have more lawyers to the square mile than one could crowd into the whole of London. Their lawyers are statesmen, while with us they are mostly politicians who make laws to suit party interests."

The Judge wasn't nettled a bit, as one might have expected that he would be.

"I don't know," he said, "that the difference is so great. You hear more of law in America than in the old country, because legislation has been a fixture in Europe for centuries, whereas with us in the States laws have to be made and adjusted to fit constantly changing conditions due to expansion by immigration, and the development of new industries. The suit of clothes that fits the growing boy or the young man won't do for the middle-aged or the old. Our Constitution covers the demands of justice and equity in principle, but growth of the citizenry demands adjustment. An Englishman lives according to the standard of custom set for him by his elders. He doesn't know that the custom is simply the translation of law, nor even that there is a law, until he breaks it. We in America meet at every step the newcomer who, escaped from an old cage whither he cannot return, selects his new roost according to his liking and feels as though he now owns the world. This leads to license which needs, checking. It makes our public law somewhat unsteady when compared with that of other countries where the average man enjoys well-tested and long-established ways."

"That's all right in England," interposed a genial sort of neighbor whose prosperous air suggested the Gaelic contractor. "But what about British rule for Ireland? England doesn't seem to know any liberty of law there." Nobody took up the objection, and there was a momentary lull in the conversation. Then the Judge turned toward the Padre:

"What is your opinion, Professor, about our legislation—but I suppose you moralists ignore law in lieu of conscience, which is a thing one cannot easily get at so long as the Deity who is the arbiter remains out of sight. But, then, I suppose He is presumed to speak through Holy Mother Church. I mean no irreverence, Sir, yet it would be instructive as well as interesting to hear your view of 'moral intention' as compared with law."

"I don't quite understand," said the Padre. "Do you mean that we Catholic moralists substitute motive for law?"

"Why, yes—something like the maxim of the Jesuits, though repudiated by them, as I believe in theory—the end justifies."

The Padre smiled.

"Why, Judge," he said, "we priests are nothing if not students and reverers of the law. Do you know what I have been doing all morning? Just drumming the idea and necessity of law into my head and heart. Actually and literally I have been studying the various forms of law, human, divine, ceremonial and moral, natural and spiritual. I am sure I have literally and audibly repeated the idea of law to myself at the rate of a hundred and seventy times in less than five minutes."

They all laughed.

"You are not in earnest of course. But, all joking aside, I was wondering what you were getting out of that rather ponderous book which you seem to carry with you pretty much all the time. It appears to be a prayer-book or Bible. Still you don't look, if you will pardon the personality, like a sanctimonious Bible Christian of the kind that carries their religion for show."

"I mean precisely what I was saying," answered his Reverence, as he pulled me up from the cushion beside him. "This is a law book—the Bible, if you wish; for the terms are, as among the Jews, in reality nearly synonymous. But it is also a commentary on the Law, somewhat like your Chitty and Blackstone. You understand Latin, Judge, I presume, for they say you are a Harvard man, and anyhow you must have had much reading of Roman Law. Look at this."

With that the Padre turned to Prime, pointing to the One Hundred and Eighteenth Psalm, while the Judge looked important and followed the point of the chief's finger, the other men being roused to curiosity, and a little doubtful alike of the Padre's assertion and the Judge's appreciation.

"See—

Beati qui ambulant in *lege* (law)
Qui scrutantur *testimonia* (legal prescriptions)
Tu mandasti *mandata* (precepts—mandates)

THE JUDGE INVESTIGATES

Ad custodiendas *justificationes* (judicial decisions)
Verbum tuum (Thy word—i.e. word, law of God)
Judicia tua (Thy judgment, sentence)
in *æquitate* tua (law of equity);

and so forth. You see the words *sermones, eloquia, statuta, verba,* etc. are but varying terms for the one idea of law, just as in our own tongue we have the words commandment, statutes, ordinances, laws, precepts, decrees, judgments, sentence, and the like expressing merely different phases and applications of the same thought. Now if you look into your own Bible, the one hundred and nineteenth Psalm of the King James or the Revised Version of 1883, you will find this law-term mentioned at least one hundred and seventy times in as many verses. You see, it is no exaggeration to say that when one reads this Psalm—and it takes less than five minutes—one actually utters 'law' as often in the given time. Take the book and examine it for yourself."

And thus the Padre handed me over to the civil court. I felt mighty shaky, with the memory of the Spanish Inquisition before me, though quite innocent even of any heterodox Jewish leanings, if not of Hebrew alliances.

"Well, well—this is astonishing, and interesting. And so this volume you carry around is actually a commentary with the Latin Bible text. You said 'the one hundred and nineteenth Psalm in the Revised Version.' I see here it is numbered the one hundred and eighteenth."

"Yes, the numbering of these Psalms varied somewhat among the Hebrews who lived in Palestine (and who used a Hebrew text in their readings in the synagogues and temple) from that in use among the Jews who had been carried into captivity and who under foreign domination became accustomed to the reading of the Law in the Greek language. These had a translation of the Thora and of the Psalter with slight variations in division and wording. Catholics have always, like the early Christians, used and followed the latter. Luther and the reform party of the sixteenth century, cutting away from the traditions of the Roman, or Latin, Church, preferred to adopt the Palestinian mode still preserved among the Jews. It is this little point that gives them a semblance of greater antiquity, though in reality the preference of age belongs to the old Greek version which was made by Hebrew authorities in Egypt about two hundred and fifty years before Christ."

"But isn't the Hebrew of Palestinian tradition older, as being the work of Moses?"

"It would be, if the Hebrew of the Palestinian Bible had not been subjected to certain changes—few and not very important—in regard to fundamental doctrine, and in details of interpretation and adaptation to liturgical purposes. You see, the old Hebrew text in use up to and several centuries after Christ, was a text written without vowels. Only the consonants were written. Through the continuous chain of living interpreters of the synagogal schools it was comparatively easy to remember the pronunciation of this text. It was in the hands of the rabbins, and they followed a living tradition. The Greek translators in Egypt naturally drew upon this tradition and fixed it in their writing of the Greek by expressing the accepted vowel-reading of their day—the third century before the Christian era. We know from this Greek translation (the famous Septuagint) not only what meaning the Jews of that time attached to the words of the Hebrew consonantal writing preserved in the synagogue, but also how they pronounced the unwritten vowels—at least, to some extent, as expressed in proper and conventional names. Not until six centuries later, or during the fourth and subsequent centuries of the Christian era, did the Palestinian Jews affix to their Hebrew text (which by that time through lack of usage had become almost obsolete, at least outside the liturgy)—not until six centuries later, I say, did the Palestinian Jews begin to come to an agreement as to what vowels should be affixed to the text. In fact, there were differences of opinion all through the early Middle Ages, so that only in the tenth century of our era was the vowel-reading of the Hebrew Bible permanently regulated."

"And has the Hebrew Bible of today this vowel system?"

"Yes. The Jews showed great reverence for what they considered the traditional text in that they avoided tampering with it. They affixed the vowels in form of points under the consonants or indicated the reading in the margin. But you can readily see why the early Christians preferred the Greek translation made by Jews. All in all, there are no radically important differences in the two texts, and the Catholic Church as a matter of fact uses both in her liturgy."

"Which of the two did Christ use?"

"Both, if we may judge from the three hundred or more references to the old Hebrew Bible which occur in the New Testament. While in the disputes with the Pharisees Christ, as a rule, repeats the words of the Hebrew Law, there are also evident additional references in the New Testament to the Greek version used by the Jews of the dispersion in His day."

"Professor, you are making this thing very interesting. Tell me, who wrote this Psalm about the law? David?"

"Perhaps so. More probably it dates to the time of the Captivity, some two or three centuries later, when the desire of the Jewish leaders to preserve the memory of the Law among the captives in a foreign country made devices like this Psalm desirable. Probably it owes its origin in the present form to some such captive as Daniel, a well-educated Jew and zealous for the traditions of Moses. For, apart from its peculiar content, the Psalm is a singular piece of acrostic or alphabetic poetry. Each set of eight verses begins with a letter following the regular order of the Hebrew alphabet, evidently with a view of fixing the words more easily in the memory.

"The curious part of it," continued the Padre, "is that one hardly notices the repetition which, under ordinary circumstances, would pall on or fatigue the reader. In this it is perhaps indicative and symbolical of the way in which the thought of law recurs in the Church. What some of you men call a 'priest-ridden' people are Catholics who spontaneously follow the law indicated by their leaders because they breathe it in with the very atmosphere and spirit of their faith. Those who don't understand this think that the obedience of Catholics is due to coercion."

"But this evidently artificial composition could hardly be inspired, as I understand you claim for the whole Bible?"

"Why not? Nearly all the Bible is poetic in its original form. Inspired thought does not hinder rhythmic or imaginative expression. On the contrary, it seems habitual to the visionary, such as we judge the seer or prophet to have been. The Psalm was meant, no doubt, to be didactic; that is to say, expressed in a form by which the lesson of *law* was taught to the Hebrew youth. It is a sort of catechism in verse. I said that the Psalm is

THE JUDGE INVESTIGATES

arranged in octaves. In the Hebrew the first eight lines begin with the letter *A*, the second set of eight lines begins with *B*, the third with *C* (Ghimel), and so on for the twenty-two letters of the entire alphabet. Thus the Hebrew youth learnt to remember the law and its importance under all conditions of life. The *law* was of course identical with the *Word* of God, or the *will* and *way* of God; all these terms being used in that sense throughout the Psalm."

"And do you say that every priest has to read the Psalm daily?"

"Every morning. You see, it is divided among the hours of Prime, Terce, Sext and None, which correspond to the canonical service of the forenoon."[3]

I felt mighty proud when the Judge said:

"Well, I had no idea that you were carrying a *legal code* around with you in that book of yours. Much less did I think that priests generally do so when one meets them with what seems to be a prayer-book in the railway coaches or at sea. I often wondered how they could say their prayers in the crowded thoroughfares, unless it were done in a mechanical fashion and without devotion. But I understand it is merely intellectual, a sort of reminder of the principles of the laws of the Bible."

"Not that—entirely. It is a reminder of the law, but also an act of devotion, for it is accompanied by avowals to observe the law, and invocations to have the grace and will to do so. No doubt the fact that the reading is made obligatory, to be performed within a fixed period of hours, tends to the habit of mechanical recitation. But that is a defect, like all other human weaknesses. The

---

[3] Editor's Note. Before the new order of dividing the Psalter for the Canonical Hours was introduced by Pius X. At present the Psalm is said only once a week, on Sundays.

Church takes every precaution against this. See—here—the preparatory prayer which precedes each daily repetition: *ut digne, attente ac devote recitare valeam.*"

At this point a gentleman who had been sitting apart reading a book came over to the table where the discussion about me was going on. I had noticed him looking up from time to time, as if listening. He now addressed the Judge, as though he were a bit shy of the priest, yet interested in the talk.

"You are speaking of the Psalter," he said. "Why, I have just come from Leipzig, where I picked up a curious old MS. of a Psalter, the origin of which has been puzzling me. Perhaps one of you gentlemen can throw some light on the document, if I bring it down."

There was silence for a moment—and the Judge looked toward the Padre:

"Our friend here might do so," he said; "I am afraid the rest of us are not equipped for that sort of thing."

"What is your profession, Sir?" inquired the Padre. "Is your manuscript in Latin?"

"Yes, Latin, but not the Vulgate text, as I understand from one who knows about such things. I am an engraver by trader and have for some years back been collecting rare prints and curious drawings. Someone advised me to visit the old Benedictine monasteries in Switzerland, where I saw and copied a good deal from the medieval missals and lectionaries, but of course could not purchase any of the originals. Quite by accident, however, I was in a bookseller's shop when a consignment of an old library, a relic of a legacy recently sold at auction, had just been received, the Psalter among them. It is a beautiful specimen of a Gaelic MS., with the designs of early Irish art in miniatures, though more than half of the original pages are missing. But I got the copy at a bargain and am curious to know more about it. If I had had the time I should have gone to some monastery in England or Ireland to inquire about it, for the monks are probably the best authorities on these matters. We have also expert collectors in Philadelphia and New York, who should be able to throw light on the origin of the MS. Unfortunately my trunk is in the hold, and I may have some difficulty in getting it out before we land."

"Of Irish Psalters we have a great number scattered throughout the chief national and monastic libraries of Europe. St. Gall, Vienna, Berlin, Monte Cassino, Paris, and the British Museum contain fine specimens of these liturgical manuscripts," was the Padre's comment.

"I was at St. Gall and at Einsiedeln," said the engraver. "It was there that I came to know the distinctly Irish character of early art, which one could plainly recognize in the Psalter I bought. Indeed the initial figure on the first page after the cover was a cross with an inscription which I noted down, and of which I got the interpretation from one of the University professors who happened to be in Leipzig and to whom I showed the leaves. The script reads *Cross-na-Sceaptra*, which means 'Cross of the Scriptures' and refers to a peculiar form of cross used in Ireland. I was told that there is a fine specimen of the same design in front of the Cathedral at Clonmacnoise."

"Precisely," said the Padre. "The Irish were the first to open schools of learning after the Christian persecutions had ceased in the Roman Empire. While the Benedictine monks were teaching the barbarians in central Europe the first lessons in agriculture, letters, arts, the early missioners who came over from Gaul found in the Irish a most appreciative and intellectually superior people. Thus it happened that the monastic schools in Ireland became the centers of learning whither Strangers from all parts of the Continent flocked. One need only mention Agilbert, the illustrious Bishop of Paris, Egbert of Northumbria, and his disciples Wigbert and Willibrord, who later became the apostles of Friesland. Better known among the English are Chad, and the Anglo-Saxon princes Oswald, Oswy, and Aldfrith."

"What did they teach in the Irish schools that brought men to them from the Continent of Europe? Anything besides these psalters, of which there are, you say, numerous hand- wrought copies, among the old treasures of our libraries? All I have seen anywhere of this type of literature," said the engraver, who appeared to be a well-to-do and a fairly educated man, "seems to be rather devotional than anything else—is it not?"

"Devotional and at the same time broadly and distinctly didactic. These books are generally just what you see in this volume"—and he held me up to them—me, the Totum which he said contains a whole university course in principles of law, philosophy, history, and literature.

"I thought you said that book of yours was a Latin Bible," came an interjection from the Judge.

"So it is. But much more. It contains at the same time an interpretation and varied illustrations of the Biblical wisdom. The fact is that the study of the Bible in Ireland from the sixth century on became the basis of the divers secular as well as religious intellectual disciplines. And later on these were expanded under the Frankish schools of the Carlovingian period and became the beginnings of the great universities, Padua, Paris, Oxford, which furnished the inspiration for the study of the highest culture and art.

"What you see condensed in this book," continued the Padre, "which is the daily companion of the Catholic priest everywhere—is indeed the Bible, commented on to serve as the most complete though rudimentary code of legislative wisdom, and of the art of right living, the foundation of all ethical culture. At the same time it is the most perfect model of historical writing. It relates things as the writers witnessed them, without eulogy or minimizing. Its greatest, heroes, like Abraham, Moses, David, Peter, are pictured with all their faults as well as their virtues.

"Even today the didactic books of the Bible and the historical experiences related to serve as illustrations, offer a key to the solution of our social problems, with far more security than you will find among the doctrinaires of domestic, social and political science."

The Padre stopped, but I could see that he had made the men who stood by, thoughtful. I had a hard time to keep from turning a somersault, and my leaves fluttered in the draft that swept through the room, with elation at the appreciation of my merits. I shall never forget it, and I resolved then and there to do my best to further the beatification of the Padre when it comes to that, for I understand of course that priests are meant to be canonized, and we Breviaries shall be called to witness against the wiles of the 'advocatus diaboli.'

"No," resumed the Father, "there is no branch of human learning—that can serve a practical purpose—but finds its doctrine outlined in the wisdom of the Bible. And indeed that is the sole reason for its universal acceptance as a guide in life among all classes, and the best of men, in every nation and every age since its existence.

The shout "Man overboard" broke up our confab, and

the Padre with the rest rushed out on deck despite the rain. It proved a false alarm. One of the sailors had fallen off the midmast in attempting to adjust some ropes, and was unconscious. The Padre bent over him, and gave him conditional absolution, making the Sign of the Cross over him, for he had seen the tattooed crucifix on the poor fellow's left arm and took him to be a Catholic. The ship doctor said he thought the boy would recover, though he was badly shaken.

V. The Totum Gives a Tip to the Preacher

On the following Sunday the Padre was to have service. It was to be simply a sermon and prayers. Few of the passengers were Catholics, and would likely have attended Mass if there had been one.

An important part in the service fell to me, the Totum. I had to provide the Gospel, and gave the Padre some points for his sermon, from my Homily by St. John Chrysostom. It was fine. They all listened with reverent attention as he introduced me, interpreting in English my noble Roman sentences, for the people were of course unlettered—heathens most of them, to whom things had to be made plain, as to children. He told them that he was translating for them the very words and language which St. Paul used to the Romans, though the Apostle of the Gentiles usually spoke Greek when in learned circles. And St. Chrysostom—well, he couldn't be excelled. I think the Padre made quite an impression. Later on, one of the men seeing me lying quietly on the table in the dining salon, where I had been while the Padre was talking with a lady, very gingerly lifted the lapel of my overcoat and looked at the front page. Evidently he was puzzled—"That ain't no Bible," he quipped, and then dropped me as if I had the smallpox. I was glad to see the heretic frightened. What did he know about the Bible and St. Chrysostom? Lack of academic education as well as want of real religion.

There was a concert in the evening. The proceeds were for the Sailors' Hospital Fund. I was not present because the Padre feared there might be frivolity in such mixed company; but I could hear from my place on the traveling bag in the adjoining room that he made a speech —and how they applauded! Where he got his discourse from I don't know, for he hadn't consulted me at all, though he rarely preaches or speaks in public without drawing his inspirations in some way or other from the Breviary. My sapiential books are really wonderful; they touch almost every subject from driving a good bargain to warning against hard drinking or indiscriminate love-making. But sometimes I am neglected. "Bonum mihi quia humiliasti me," I say.

Tomorrow we are to land. I am glad, for somehow things were unsteady during the past two weeks, and I actually had several narrow escapes from slipping overboard, as the Padre always insisted upon taking me out on deck. Of course I can swim, but still it would have been unpleasant to have to live on salt water perhaps for days. I belong to the 'drys,' being a T.B., which forbids water, except holy water, and that comes in drops and under the name of spirits.

So here I am locked up in the handbag, though on top, as a mark of respect for my dignity, and also for convenience' sake.

We were up early, and the Padre and I had a chat.

Funny, they all stood in line to have their hand baggage examined. When it came to us the revenue officer saw me, first thing in the bag; then touched his cap and said, "All right, Father. You have nothing that is dutiable." It was glorious to see how they all respected me, a foreigner, in this great country. Perhaps they remembered that it was Columbus, a countryman of mine, who first discovered it.

VI. The Breviary in the Police Station

I really don't know what happened, for I was shut up in the Padre's valise, with those nastily soiled clothes, hair brush, cigar case, and a lot of second-hand books and catalogues. The only decent company was a silk cassock, some clean handkerchiefs, and a new railroad timetable. The first glimpse of light and release from the stuffy atmosphere came to me with a shock, when I found myself in the hands of a New York policeman. After irreverently fumbling with my flyleaf and examining my face he said:

"Begorra, Captain, this thing belongs to a priest, and by the same token one who is as poor as a church mouse, unless the guy who took it from him was before us in emptying it of a pocketbook."

"Any name?"

"Yes, in the book here—the Rev. J. Hogan, D. D.—that's all."

"Did you see anything of the fellow who dropped it?"

"Yes, one of those chaps who hang round the station. I noticed him lifting it from a seat, near the ticket office, where I now remember seeing a priest waiting in line. I suspected the fellow was taking somebody else's bag, and I was making for him, when he spied me and dropped it—losing himself in the crowd at the door."

"Well, leave it here. We'll inquire about the owner.

IN THE POLICE STATION

Give me that book." And with this I was chucked on the desk in the office.

After a while I heard a voice:

"Say, Shorty, come here. Go over to the Cathedral, Madison Avenue, with this card and ask whether the clergy there know of the priest by the name on it. Get his address, if you can. Say we recovered a bag—taken from a priest at the railroad station, and we're looking for the owner. Go at once and get back here before I go off duty at noon."

Meanwhile another policeman came in. He had sergeant's stripes.

"What's this, Captain?"

"Oh, a priest's bag which Muldoon saw a hard nut carrying off at the station while the owner had put it down to get his ticket."

"A priest's? What's in it?"

"Not much, except truck."

"How'd you get the name?"

"From that book on top."

Now here was another item that gave an indication of my importance. If it hadn't been for me they couldn't have recognized the Padre's property. It's great to be a Breviary, a Totum. The night-shirt couldn't have done it, for there are Hogans galore in the world. And the handkerchiefs with their puny initials couldn't tell anything about the Padre, though they had took him often enough by the nose."

"Seems to be a prayer-book—and new."

"Prayer-book, you stupid! Why, that's what they call a Missal. Look at it; it's all Latin. That's where priests get to know things, and the power to work miracles. I haven't been to church for a long time—but I know that much. Did ye ever see them read it over sick people?"

"I seen them read it in the subway and once at a picnic. But I don't know that that's the place to say your prayers; and if it works miracles, they'd no doubt rather use it in church to raise the collection, for they are strong after the money."

"See here, Mike. It's easily seen you aren't much of a Catholic. Neither am I, if it comes to church-going. But my ancestors were decent chaps in the old country, and I heard my father say that there were three priests among them, and a third cousin who was a bishop in Ireland. Of course they need money, and it's a wonder they get it with fellows like you and me fighting shy of the collections. If it weren't for my wife there'd be no chance to get the boys to the Sisters' school. And we know that the toughs that come our way in the police station would be a lot better off if they had had some religion instead of just getting their wits sharpened in the public schools."

In a half hour "Shorty" returned.

"They know the priest all right, if the owner is a priest. I told them about the book, and they said that he must have just returned from Europe, and that he would probably call on the Archbishop. If so, they will send for the valise; otherwise it might be returned to him directly. They gave me his address."

"Well, now, isn't it wonderful? Here is a priest who belongs out West, coming back from Europe, and they know all about him at the Cathedral. There must be more than ten thousand priests in the United States. How do they keep tabs on them?"

"Oh, the young Father who saw me said: 'I'll just look in the *Catholic Directory* for the name.' But while he was away another priest came through the vestibule and asked me whom I wanted to see. I told him my errand, and he knew at once the man I was looking for."

"No doubt he is a prominent clergyman."

"One would hardly think so from his baggage—pretty poor stuff, except the new prayer-book. All the same, the Catholic Church is a great organization. As we used to learn in Sunday School—*One, Holy, Catholic, Apostolic.* I got a corker of a cigar from the Father, who said it was very good of us to send the inquiry."

"Trust our Gotham for a decent police force!"

VII. A R*IDE* IN THE P*ULLMAN* C*AR*

You should have seen the Padre when he got me back. He had called at the Cathedral, I heard, but was obliged to leave New York by the night train, and they sent for us to the police station. The first thing he looked for on opening the bag was me. Then he examined my heart, the insides. We had missed a whole day's company, and I know he must have thought of me after we boarded the train—a Pullman sleeper, which was insufficiently lighted for reading. I could hear him rattle the old beads—a sorry consolation—while he could not talk to me.

Early next morning—after the Padre, barefooted, had taken a perfunctory ablution—he came back to the berth, and sat down with me. Though first he got to his knees and made a big Sign of the Cross, perhaps to shy off the darkey "boots" who seemed anxious to get him out of the passage. We did not at first notice the heavy snoring of the fat man in the upper berth. After a little it became annoying and interfered with our conversation. Anyhow, it wasn't easy to keep up our dignity in the cramped position below, and the rhythmic booming from above diverted attention and demonstrated the incongruity of our acting "digne, attente, ac devote," as we had said we would do. The Padre, with a jerk, shut me up, put on his boots, and walked me into the next car, which was a parlor coach. Now I knew he didn't affect much comfort in traveling, for I heard him say so on the way to Brussels when we were not yet very well acquainted with each other. He was a democrat, and preferred to journey, whenever possible, like a missionary "per pedes apostolorum," or in a popular conveyance at any rate. Many times afterward, when the seminarians and professors went on excursions into the country, and some of the men ordered a wagon because they feared the fatigue, he would make fun of them: "Hi in equis, hi in curribus, nos autem in nomine Domini." However, night travel for a long distance had made our taking a parlor car necessary.

We had just settled down when a man and a woman with two children entered the coach and took the vacant seats right near us. They had Hebrew faces, which I rather liked, because, I suppose, of my ancestry; but the children made such a racket, right round about us, that it became quite irritating, and I could that the Father, who looked straight into my face, was annoyed. Of course there was no use pretending to pray or even to read. The only thing we could do was to change places, but that was not so easy, because here the seats were reserved. Finally the Padre stopped the conductor and asked if there were any seats in the day coaches ahead. "Why, yes," said the trainman, "plenty of seats. Go right on, next to the smoker."

The Padre had finished Prime in the sleeper amid the trumpet-like accompaniment of snoring from the upper berth. Now, that we found a restful corner near an open window, with the crisp fresh morning air blowing in, I couldn't help fluttering with the joy of it, despite the Father's thumbs trying to hold me down. We had still several hours to ride, so that there was no reason to hurry; hence I was not disposed to close my eyes, though my motions disconcerted the Padre a bit, I think, for he just clapped down the morocco cap over me, poking one finger of the left hand between my ribs, near the Office of *Con-non-Pon*. Then he began to reflect, as was his wont every morning. Today he meditated on the *Capitulum*. It was some satisfaction to know that I was in his mind anyhow, though I was muzzled for the moment.

Justum deduxit Dominus per vias rectas (Sap.10:10). I could hear him reflect. He sometimes meditates in the Davidic fashion, mumbling to himself. *Justum*, that is—if you try to do the will of God, namely that which is His right and your duty, which is the *jus* expressed by the law, the Commandments, the precepts of the Church, the canons and the rubrics that safeguard due reverence for the sacred functions, the sacramental rites and ceremonies, why, then the Lord will smooth your way through all kinds of difficulties. *Deduxit*—He has so done in the past with His servants. But in the Hebrew text in which the Book of Wisdom was originally written, the past tense often stands for the future. Hence the Latin reading might be *deducet*—He will lead him—and is an assurance of confidence in God amid the diffidence urged by purely earthly conditions.

So the future and the past, in the old Hebrew language, the tongues of fire in which the Holy Ghost spoke on Pentecost to the Apostles, are alike in their appeal, because that appeal comes from the Lord who knows no distinction of time, being ever present, eternal.

Through the *vias rectas* of the Law we reach the kingdom of heaven—*et ostendit illi regnum Dei*. They are straight ways, at times a bit hard under foot, that is, to our earthly feelings. Yet they are right and sure, because, as the word *rectas* implies, directed by God, toward the *regnum,* that is to say right ruling, both in the pastoral administration and in any other sphere of government.

Besides this it increases personal holiness, for that is what is meant by the *scientia sanctorum* in the next sentence: *"Et dedit*(dabit) *illi scientiam sanctorum."* This gives dignity to the priest in all the departments of his apostolic labor. It supplies the prudence in the confessional and in the direction of the faithful.

Here the Padre paused—*"Honestavit ilium in laboribus, et complevit labores illius* "Dear Lord," I heard him say under his breath, "Thou knowest the difficult task that lies before me in the direction of the seminary. To guide the young aspirants to the priesthood in the way of the responsibility that awaits them. As their habits are fashioned during the eight or nine years while they are under the immediate control of the ecclesiastical authorities, and still full of the enthusiasm with which they followed Thy call, so will they be later. As they are then, so will be the flocks confided to their care. Nor would my own efforts avail, even if I were perfectly devoted, bending all my energies upon the duties of a superior, unless I had the cooperation of the right quality of men. The professors, the members of the domestic service, need all be disposed to work in harmony. One faithless official or even menial, who connives underhand with incipient departure from discipline, may prove the germ of a canker that corrupts the others from within. The selection of priests to fill the void in the faculty and the organization of studies (which devolves on me for the next year) gives anxiety. There is N., a bright theologian, a genial fellow, but indolent, fond of amusement, having altogether a rather low estimate of that ascetical spirit and self-restraint which is such an essential factor in preserving the aspirations for devotion, zeal, self-sacrifice, without which a priest, even if he does good work, is merely a hireling. I have doubts too about young E. He is willing and docile, but weak, lacks character, does not bridle his tongue—a bad asset for a teacher and a danger to his maintaining the respect of the students; then his social proclivities, leaving the seminary routine on the slightest pretext, and staying out rather than coming home for a decent game of cards—Lord, these things clog for me, the rector, advance per *vias rectas,* unless Thou come to my aid."

Et complevit (complebit) *labores illius.* Well, if I only go on, fearless of human respect, keeping the *Jus* before me, the Lord will fill up all that is wanting to me in knowledge, foresight, courage—by giving to His servant the *scientia sanctorum.*

"Padre, the half hour of meditation is up," I felt like shouting, as we came to a station stop, for the dear old saint had kept me in darkness all the while, never getting beyond that chapter in Prime, which by the way is called "Lectio brevis." He ought to keep the rubrics, but then I heard him answering my mutterings by: "The chapter in Prime is taken from the hour of None." There he has me, for that is quoting rubrics and allows perhaps protraction for three full hours. He must know, because he taught rubrics for some years, and I think will do so again, even though he has been made rector of the seminary.

Now for Terce, Sext and None. I was mortally afraid the Padre would begin his meditations again when he came to the *Beatus vir— qui post aurum non abiit, nec speravit in pecunia*—but he passed right on. I had nothing to fear from the chapter at Sext—*Cor suum tradidit ad vigilandum diluculo*—for I know by this time that he needs no alarm clock to wake him. He is a good sport, and rises *diluculo* all right, jumping promptly out into the cold bath. And as for the *in conspectu Altissimi deprecabitur,* the fact that he does handle me "pie, attente ac devote" is an indication that we are no lip-servers or prayer machines, for of course in that matter he has to have me to keep him in order.

VIII. A Chat with Sophia

Little Hours over, the Padre suddenly peered into my face as if he had forgotten something. I know he likes to contemplate my beauty, and I confess—I may say it without conceit—that I think he could hardly find a better subject; for what else would make them take photo-copies of me, several impressions—at Tours—and put the diocesan seal on my lapels as a sort of hallmark bestowed exclusively on Totums of the gilt-edged élite? I could feel the distinction, especially while in the forced company of those second-hand volumes which the Padre had picked up at the antiquary's bookstand in Brussels. They were shabby, and none of them could claim a pedigree of Romano-Gallican descent, with the Patriarchal strain that flowed in my veins. Well, he likes the looks of me, and sometimes keeps feasting his eyes on the lines of my countenance. Just now, I suspect, it was the Sap. X (wisdom excellent) that attracted him. From it the *lectio brevis* at Prime and the *capitulum* at None in the Con-non-Pon office are taken. Sure enough! He began to read. After a little while he went back for his portmanteau, and having fumbled through its contents, he brought out—what do you think—a Greek tome, Elzevir edition. I almost got jealous, but then I soon saw it was a respectable-looking female by the name "Sophie" (Sophia). She belongs to the Bible; so we are relations, though there had been no formal introduction. The cover was rather old and worn, but it bore the marks of having been distinguished at one time. The Father said it was "antique."

I wondered what he wanted with the Greek Bible. Later I found out. The Greek books of the Bible are, as it were, detectives of original texts to which scholars refer, respectable investigators, of course. They are employed to cross-examine you, your words, and get at your intentions. The Padre wanted to find out where my Sap. came from, and here was an old lady who knew all the facts; and who was disposed to give out, so that he could trace every statement of mine and its original meaning. I only know ecclesiastical Latin. Some of my parts are in the style of St. Jerome, who was a pretty fine classical scholar. But this Sap. X is African Latin. It is not bad, only a bit Italian. In fact they call it still *Itala* Latin. St. Jerome was a skeptic in Greek matters. He thought that the Holy Ghost spoke Hebrew, and only grudgingly allowed that what are called the deutero-canonical books of the Bible were inspired. This Sap. is the short for *Sapientiæ Liber,* as the Vulgate styles it. Formerly it stood for *Sapientia Salomonis* in the Latin Bibles. Whether Solomon wrote it—which would have been Hebrew—is very doubtful.

Probably the present text is of later date. Nevertheless, it embodies what was accepted among the Jews of the dispersion, that is outside Palestine, as the wisdom of Solomon, when in his earlier years he hearkened to the inspirations of Jahweh. Most likely the book was written in Greek, as we still have it in famous ancient manuscripts such as the Vatican, Sinaitic, and Alexandrine (Egyptian) texts.

It is a wonderful book. You get the temptation to be high-browed in such company unless you remember Solomon and how he ended. This Book of Wisdom contains the entire philosophy of life in its speculative and historical aspects. For the man of the world it solves all the problems that confront him in his earthly career, and it is here that the cleric gets that prudence of the serpent which protects him on the one hand against the deceits of men, while it furnishes him with that superior wisdom by which he discerns truth and is enabled to guide others.

The Padre soon became engrossed in the old tome. Sometimes he looked puzzled, as if he suspected me, his Latin Totum, of mistranslation, despite my certificates from the Cardinals and Sacred Congregation. But I don't care. I am Roman, and have the Pope on my side.

IX. Arrival, on Terra Firma. The Totum Pays a Visit to a Convent of Nuns

The Padre had been clearing his glasses several times as though he wanted more light. He was at the Gospel of St. Luke, which I explain, though it is simple enough, as St. Gregory says: "aperta est vobis lectio recitata; sed ne aliquibus ipsa ejus planities alta fortasse videatur, eam sub brevitate transcurrimus." Now whether it was growing darkness around us, or the shaking of the car, which made him nod again and again, the dear old professor went off, dozing right over me so that I was all the time in peril of falling to the floor. It was in my mind to wake him up with "beatus ille servus quem, cum venerit Dominus ejus, invenerit vigilantem," when the conductor of the train came in and noisily shouted: "Next stop, Central. All out! Change cars for the North and West!" It really was annoying, for though I had been very quiet, the Padre now jerked me with a "Shut up" air, as if I were the offending railroad officer. But immediately he made the Sign of the Cross, showing that he was sorry for the rough treatment; and, really, the slaps I get from him on such occasions are not very hard; they are more like those the bishop gives to children when they are being confirmed. Anyhow, I have been knocked about much more roughly since the Padre gave me away to a young Irish deacon. But of these experiences later.

After being unceremoniously pushed into a corner of the valise, I found myself once more in the ill-smelling company of the tobacco pouch, strangely out of keeping with the odor of sanctity arising from the saint mentioned in the lesson of the day.

Muzzled, and in the dark, I don't know what happened until the Padre held me up in the amber light of a shaded kerosene lamp which revealed a cosy room with holy pictures—all, except one, much larger than the rest, over the mantelpiece. It was evidently the portrait of some bishop, with a large pectoral cross and the left hand supporting the chin as if the amethyst on the ring-finger were doing some thinking. We studied the face for a little while, after which the Padre put me down on the table as one might say: "You have seen enough. Not very handsome. But then he is not your bishop nor mine."

Now I know this sounds almost irreverent; and the Padre is never that. But once, since then, I was in a rectory where the curates were playing cards, and when the pastor came in they asked him to "take a hand." He didn't, though.

"The Bishop will be here next week on visitation," he said, pointing to a portrait on the wall, "and he will be asking sundry questions as to how the curates behave. Being a conscientious man, I shall have to tell him about this pinochle playing of my assistants; and I fear he will suspend Father Larry at once because this is not the only bad habit I shall have to report about him. As for the rest of you, he is sure to remember this waste of precious time, when it comes to the next promotion for a vacant rectorship."

They laughed as though they didn't believe the Father Rector was in earnest. Anyhow, they said that as long as they were not playing for money it was a harmless recreation; and the pastor was evidently pleased with them. After the game was over they fell to talking about the bishop's coming; and it was then I learned for the first time that one might be a bishop without being exactly a saint. They didn't seem at all afraid of him, at least while he was absent, albeit when he actually came later on they all knelt down very reverently and kissed the amethyst on his finger; and Father Larry never said a word while the bishop was at dinner, though he could talk well enough, and people liked his preaching. However, I must go on with what happened to the Padre.

X. A Talk with the Abbess. The Padre Asks the Advice of the Totum

After he had made his ablutions, the Padre put on a clean Roman collar and took a glance in the looking-glass. From the way he rubbed his chin I knew that he did not feel quite comfortable, for he hadn't shaved that morning. Just then there was a gentle knock at the door, and in answer to his "Come in" two nuns entered, smiling a greeting and promptly kneeling to get his blessing. One of them was an elderly lady, of sweetly grave countenance and refined manner, who in addressing the Padre at once revealed the fact that the other her younger companion, was a relation of the priest's, for she called her "your niece," adding "since you professed her she has been a dear child and has made good progress in her studies of Latin and Scripture, as you wanted her to do."

They talked of the journey—mine and the Padre's—though it was evident they were more interested in his doings than in mine. They never adverted to the fact that I had an introduction from several cardinals, nor to the Pope's letter on my front page. But I am getting used to neglects of this kind, though the Padre knows very well that he could not do without me even for a day, unless he were sick or something, and had to call for that Rosary nurse of his. Finally the Reverend Mother, in taking leave with her companion, said:

"Tomorrow is Our Lady's feast. You will stay with us, of course, and give us Benediction after Mass—and might we ask you for a little ferverino on the feast?"

When they had gone the Padre scratched his head. The ferverino meant that he should have to give a talk to the nuns in the morning. That was not so easy. They were a contemplative and teaching Order, under the direction of the Jesuit Fathers in the adjoining church, as I learnt next day. While he was looking about, I heard him mutter to himself: "One needs to be careful with these nuns."

He sat down under the lamp, with me right before him on the table. It was evident he meant to consult me about this talk to the Community. If he had been at home he would probably have consulted some book in his library to furnish material for a thoughtful talk to the Religious, who remember things and discuss what the priest says, among themselves. But now I was the only help, apparently.

At first he looked me over in a sort of musing fashion. Then he turned to the "Officium de B. Maria V.," as I knew he would. "Specie tua et pulchritudine tua" caught his eye; then "Quasi oliva speciosa in campis." He was getting into the "hortus conclusus." It was curious to see how he became interested. Finally he picked up a sheet of letter paper with the convent address on it, and jotted down:

Oliva—the olive, symbol of Our Blessed Lady. The olive gives oil, which is
   1. *food,* rich *nourishment* for the body;
   2. a source of *illumination;*
   3. *medicine* for healing wounds;
   4. an *ointment* to give physical strength, producing flexibility of muscle and growth of tissue.

Application: Mary, Virgin, Mother, gives to us Jesus, the fruit of her chaste womb. From her we receive Christ the Anointed, who becomes our food in the Blessed Eucharist. *Oliva fructifera*—Mary, the fruitful olive tree is not only the mother that nourishes us; she also is the *light* that guides—the Star of the Sea illuminating the darkness of our earthly journey. Again she is the *Salus infirmorum,* our health in sickness, warding off death, while soothing our pains—our *Consolatrix afflictorum.* Finally, Mary is our comfort, our *strength* in the battle against the tempter.

Here was an outline of a conference which suggested abundant application to Our Lady as the Mother of Grace, sustaining, enlightening, healing, and comforting in the struggle toward perfection. Probably the nuns had heard all this before.

But there was the next image in that wonderful enclosed garden. "Quasi Palma exaltata in Cades." The Father remembered the Hebrew word for the palm tree (thamar), symbol of queenly grace, lifting its head up to heaven amid the oasis in the desert.

"Cades," the Padre mumbled, "means *sacred.* This stands for the soul growing in holiness amidst the holy solitude of the religious life, for the palm is the image of the chaste beauty, the fair grace of virginity, sheltered within the sanctuary of the convent. It was in Cades, so named by Moses, the Hebrew lawgiver, that Aaron's tabernacle was raised, where the ark was kept containing the manna. This heavenly food in the Ark of the Covenant was the symbol of the receptacle of the Incarnate Word, Mary the Immaculate, in whose bosom Christ rested—'Creator omnium requievit in tabernaculo meo.' As Cades remained the central sanctuary, the place of the oracle, during the wanderings of the Hebrews after they had received the law on Mount Sinai, before they entered into the promised land, so Mary the Immaculate remains the 'Seat of Wisdom,' the 'Mother of Good Counsel' to the children elect of her religious family. It was in Cades, too, where the 'Holy Well' (Ain Qadis), the wonderful 'Fons salutis' for the children of Israel, flowed with health-giving grace, when all other sources in the desert around them had dried up. It was at Cades that Mary, the sister of Moses, was buried, associating her name not only with that of her brother, the savior of his people, but also with Mary, the Mother of Christ—'Mater Salvatoris.'"

It was getting late, and I was going to say:

"Padre, that is enough; for you are perspiring and leaving ugly thumb-marks on me. Go to bed, and sleep over what you have read. Leave the rest to the Holy Ghost, since we two have done our best. You need only expand the matter and put my promptings into speech. Remember, 'hominis est præparare animam, et Domini gubernare linguam.' "

The Padre had become interested, however, and, as I found later, when his mind was once fixed on developing an idea, there was no holding him back. Of course, as long as he was really in love with me I felt satisfied and could hardly blame him. Sometimes I have been in the hands of clerics who just treated me as if I were nothing but a common prayer-book, or a school manual which one wants to get through with as quickly as possible. But the professor knew better. Besides, my companionship gave him an opportunity to air his familiarity with Hebrew and Greek, a knowledge which, I sometimes suspect, he is a little proud of. But then I often remind him that, after all, his knowledge is nothing compared to that of the great Fathers like Chrysostom, Leo, or Gregory, with whom I have been associated from birth.

" 'Quasi cedrus in Libano . . . et quasi platanus juxta aquam in plateis,' " the Padre went on quietly. "The cedar (Hebrew 'Erez) is the juniper tree. It was always regarded as a sacred plant by the ancients, who burnt it in sacrifice, as if it were incense; because it is aromatic. It keeps things associated with it from corruption. Moths or rodent destroyers of textile fabrics are shy of its fragrance. Being burnt in sacrifice at the annual dedications, it has become the symbol of self-sacrifice in the service of religion.

"It was used exclusively to light the great fane-fires on top of the hills to celebrate national victories," said the Professor, talking to himself. "Thus the cedar has become the image of Our Lady of Victory. She is the light, bright as the sun, which shines forth to the Christian world amid the darkness of sin, and as a result of the sacrifice, a burnt offering consumed as a holocaust at the foot of the Cross."

Then the Father remembered that, while the cedar was commonly used among the ancient peoples in sacrifices to the Deity, it served the special purpose of decoration among the Hebrews. The prophets Isaiah, Ezechiel, Amos, each record visions of the future glory of their people by the figure of a lofty cedar tree. More frequently than marble or granite was its wood used in symbolic carvings atop the lofty pillars at the entrance gates of sanctuary and temple. Popularly the cedar was spoken of as the prince among trees; and the proverbial grove of Mount Libanus stood for everything that was exalted in the eyes of the Hebrew. Its resin-filled grain admitted of an extraordinary polish, like that of ivory, and its aroma was supposed not only to be pleasant, but also health-giving. No wonder that the inspired writers should see in the cedar an image of the future glory of Israel, the Mother of Christ—"Tu gloria Jerusalem, tu lætitia Israël—in electis meis mitte radices."

The Padre kept on in his meditation half aloud. "Sicut cypressus in monte Sion.' Ah, *Ek-shamen!* It is the precious oil that flows from the cypress which brings it into the category of the olive. It lacks indeed the fruit of the olive, but it gives its unctious sap directly from the trunk and branches. It differs from the popular olive in that it is 'semper virens,' an evergreen, whose life symbolizes the immortality, the incorrupt passing of Our Lady assumed into heaven. She is bodily transplanted into paradise."

No doubt the Padre would have gone on meditating

and taking notes until early morning if something had not gone wrong with the lamp. Either the wick was burnt out, or else there was not much more oil left. Anyhow the light went gradually down, and we had to stop. I don't think he said his prayers very devoutly before he went to bed, for he was too excited.

XI. What Happens in the Chapel, and in the "Enclosed Garden" of Our Lady

The next morning we had a grand celebration. I was in the sacristy all the time, next to a gorgeous cope. And there were two little altar boys looking very prim and important in their red and white gowns and mantelettas. The nuns and the children sang at the Mass in a way which must have done the heart of St. Gregory good, though he is now no doubt quite used to the angelic choirs who sing the Missa de Angelis without fault. But the climax of beautiful singing was when after Mass they all chanted the "Salve Regina," which is one of my favorite anthems. Indeed, I call it my special salute to the Blessed Virgin; and anyone who talks with me officially, knowing my position with the court of Rome, has to repeat it, sometimes more than once a day, from first Vespers of Trinity Sunday until None of the Saturday before Advent. The nuns must have known all that, though the Father, I am sure, had said nothing to them about it, which showed that my reputation is world-wide.

If you ask me how I got possession of that anthem, I can only say that it was impressed upon me from the very first. Someone said that it was composed by a German monk nearly a thousand years ago. He was lame and stooped in the shoulders, which nevertheless had a fine head on them. He lived in a monastery on an island, Reichenau, of Lake Constance, and spent his days in study and writing until he died in 1054. They tell wonderful things about his learning. He knew, it seems, Latin and Greek and Hebrew and Arabic almost like his mother-tongue. Among the treasures in the MS. library of the old Benedictine monastery are books written by him on mathematics, astronomy, music, philosophy and theology, and a collection of beautiful poems, mostly about the Blessed Virgin, and many of them, no doubt, composed by himself. His name was Hermann Wolverad, although his contemporaries knew him better by the name "Contractus," the cripple, because he walked bent and was also of an humble disposition. In some books his name is given as Herimanus Augiensis, perhaps because his father was a count and Lord of Altshausen. But I don't know much of him, for he kept to himself and did not seem to care for human praise or thanks. He also composed the beautiful hymn, "Alma Redemptoris Mater," and, being an artist, used to make all kinds of musical instruments for the monks, and even clocks to keep them punctual in their obedience to the monastery rules. He must have been a saint, though he is not in my calendar.

    I forgot to say that the concluding part, that is, the invocation of the "Salve Regina," is generally attributed to St. Bernard of Clairvaux, who on coming into the Cathedral at Speyer on Christmas eve, when the monks were chanting the hymn as a processional, raised his clarion voice at the end, and added "O clemens, o pia, o dulcis Virgo Maria." This invocation was thenceforth kept as part of the hymn as though it had been inspired, for St. Bernard was greatly respected, and acted at the time as Apostolic Delegate on visitation to the abbey.

I remember now that, later on, the Padre told the students at the seminary where he and I had charge of the liturgy class, that the "Salve Regina" was very popular as an evening song in all the countries of Europe. The guilds and confraternities used to sing it in chorus in the open marketplace. In time it became the regular conclusion of the evening devotions in the churches, so that the Vesper devotion itself came to be known as the "Salve." In France they still call the Benediction service by the name of "Salut," owing to the practice of chanting the "Salva Regina" in connection with the night devotions. The Spanish and Italian sailors are very fond of the hymn, and carol it while pulling their oars, much as the Neapolitans chant the "Santa Lucia." I think it is in that way it got to the Indians, who learned it from the mariners that came over with Columbus; for some of the native Indian tribes seem to have it as an old tradition among their folk-tunes.

And do you know that while the nuns and pupils were singing all in unison, the strains of the organ—or was it violin and viola—made a wonderfully festive accompaniment to the singing? From what the Padre afterward said to the Reverend Mother about the beautiful instrumental setting, I knew that it was Pergolesi's composition. Otherwise I like nothing so much for the hymn as the exquisite plain-chant air, which is also attributed to my German friend Hermannus Contractus.

At breakfast, which the Padre took without me, the Sister superior came to say that if it were agreeable to His Reverence, as he was not to leave until the following morning, they would have the conference in the evening before Benediction. I could see that this pleased him, for he immediately asked to be allowed to go to the library,

WHAT HAPPENS IN THE CHAPEL 59

saying that he should see his niece after the dinner-hour, when she would most likely be free from school routine.

The Sister librarian came in due time and brought the Padre to the convent library. It was a fine hall, with all sorts of busts of heroes and authors, having inscriptions, and there were desks and catalogue cases, everything in prim style, as I have often seen it in convents since then.

Naturally I could not be left behind; so I stayed with the party, although I knew very well that the Padre had said all his Little Hours before Mass, and that his meditations were rather awry and mixed up with the conference to be had on Our Blessed Lady. What he was really after was the "compositio loci." For the "hortus conclusus," with its palms and cedars and delights, as I had described them to him in the office of Our Lady, suggested a suitable background for his talk to the nuns. His mind was set on that, and instead of making resolutions before Mass and aspirations at his thanksgiving, as he usually did, he transferred all the resolutions and aspirations to them. I do not mind it much, so long as we had to do our task in collaboration and I was not being neglected. I know that such distractions as just now possessed the Padre, while he was apparently about his Master's business, could be repaired later on by acts of contrition which he was sure to make. Moreover, I was myself anxious to please the nuns. One of them had very gingerly taken me up in the morning while the Padre was at breakfast, and examined my size. As she took my measure, I knew that I was to get a nice black overcoat which would keep my decorations from being tarnished.

When the librarian had left us after a general orientation of the departments in the library, the Padre laid me on one of the desks and got interested in the

Botany section. What he apparently wanted was to verify his notes of the previous evening; and then to find out all about nard and myrrh and balsam and cinnamon.

He looked me up: "Nardus mea dedit suavitatem odoris." The exquisite odor of nard comes from a certain herb which exudes oil. It grows originally in the Himalaya Mountains, whence it had been transplanted to Palestine. The richest yield is from its root, which shows that the forces hidden below the ground are, as a rule, the strongest; just as virtue which hides in humility is most effective and permeates. It lasts, while the clamorous glorification of earthly heroics vanishes after flashing successes. Little is said in the New Testament about Our Blessed Lady; hardly anything in direct praise of her, except by St. Luke, whose artistic temper could not pass over in silence the simple beauty of the "Immaculata" and the "Mater pulchras dilectionis." And, yet, the sounds of praise that have gone forth throughout the ages among all nations, in every city, hamlet, home, and heart of man, expressed in the devotion of artist, poet, discoverer, in the heroism of every kind and degree of genius, take their source from that hidden life of the Virgin of Nazareth. The Professor took more notes about the virtues of nardo-stachys (spikenard); and then went to "balsamum." This he found to be a liquid distilled from a kind of rosewood. It is not like our rose, though it is called "rhodium lignum." But it furnishes the attar that imparts a delicately sweet odor to all it touches. It is the symbol of devotion and corresponds to the "Rosa Mystica" which blossoms on the thorny stem of a dolorous resignation.

Another species of balm is derived from the gum of a plant now almost extinct in Palestine, though spoken of as the "balm of Gilead." It has a healing virtue, and is held as a precious cosmetic, still sometimes found in Smyrna and also in Mecca, where Oriental devotion seeks it just as the Tyrolese go in quest of the Edelweiss in secluded spots high up on the mountain sides. It is symbolic of that special contemplative devotion to Our Lady which finds its attraction on the high spiritual plains of Mount Carmel and particular Marian devotion.

It was quite time for dinner when the Padre finally got to "Quasi myrrha electa dedi suavitatem odoris." The fragrant resin collected from the myrrh plant on the Arabic and Egyptian fields is a wonderful preservative from corruption. Bitter to the taste, it is yet strangely sweet in the odors it yields. Thus it represents a foretaste of the immortality and incorruption which it is said to insure.

When one of the nuns came, respectfully waiting until he had put down the volume that told about the "flores rosarum et lilia convallium," the Padre was a little disappointed to be told that it was time for dinner. His head was so full of vegetables that I think he had quite lost his appetite. At table he was altogether distracted, which considerably puzzled the lay Sister who was serving. But when he found that her name was Sister Susanna, he seemed to lose his head entirely. He told her that the name meant "Lily" in Hebrew, and then began to describe the various kinds of lilies that grew in our gardens under the names of gladiolas, iridaceæ, and the amaryllis plants; how they all grew on a single straight stem which was like the Holy Rule; and how they made little show of foliage, but had sword-like protecting leaves that were the symbols of mortification; how the six-pointed petals symbolized the perfection of the Holy Trinity and of man as the image of God; and how the lily, especially the Annunciation lily, always bent its beautiful white head humbly down while shedding the sweet odors of its fragrant devotion silently round about it. He would have gone on but for the fact that his niece came to relieve the situation. She heartily laughed when she found that the Padre had actually eaten nothing but cauliflower, apparently digesting his botanical reflections of the morning during the process; and she promptly made him take double dessert and a glass of St. Julien before she let him say grace.

Well, it was all very delightful to think how much the Breviary could do to interest the Padre and make him hunt up things; and then how all the praises that followed the conference to the nuns in the evening were really due to me. Nor was that the end. He had a whole lot of notes which I knew he would use on future occasions to make his talks to the students and others instructive. Perhaps he would write some of them in a book; and though he might never mention (in the preface) how much of it all he got through incentives from the Totum, I should feel the satisfaction of being the real author of *The Symbolism of Biblical Plant Life* by the Rev. Dr. Hogan, Prof., etc., even though the entire praise of it came to him. Of course I am teaching him humility all the time, and ought to practice it myself by giving the credit to others while I am the B. R. Totum.

Second Part

I. THE TOTUM GETS AN AMERICAN ORDERLY

WE HAD trouble—that is, the Padre had; but he seemed somehow to blame me for it. I had often noticed that before taking me out of afternoons for a half-hour's quiet conversation about matters of the next morning, he would pick up an insignificant-looking booklet, and fumble with it as if looking, for information. Then I learnt accidentally that it was a sort of orderly which the Padre actually kept for my sake. He called it "Ordo"—I suppose for short. But in its stuck-up way on the front page it styled itself "Directorium," and pretended to be Roman like myself, albeit its Latin was barbarous, that is to say, half its words were never pronounced or even written in full. Once I got a glimpse of its insides, and found that the whole thing was nothing but purloined matter, plagiarized from my rubrics and Kalendarium.

Now, whether it was because in my humility, typified by the small print of my introductory pages, I had failed to bring the rubrics and calendar to the Padre's attention, or whether he wanted to save himself the trouble of consulting me by getting, in brief, the daily news which this glib orderly pretended to have ready for him, the "Directorium" was invariably allowed to precede me. In time I began to regard it as a sort of compliment to have this inferior always run ahead of me, for it facilitated my understanding with the Padre.

Well, today the orderly could not be found. I knew

very well where the Padre had left him—on the seat out in the convent garden where we all three had gone after the conference to the Sisters; but I would not say so. My business is to keep mum, unless the Padre wants to hear divine wisdom. The Ordo is to look after me, not I after it.

We were on the train when the Padre discovered the absence of the "Directorium." The next day was Sunday, and he had a notion that the Office was one of the Epiphany cycle which supplies the gap between the twenty-third Sunday after Pentecost and the first of Advent beginning in November. But he was not sure how many Sundays intervened. Of course I had to tell him when I saw how worried he was about that miserable orderly, who was comfortably resting on the garden seat, or perhaps in the sacristy under the eyes of the nuns. They were in the meantime, no doubt, making acts of contrition for not having discovered the pretentious little imp of a Directory in time; and they were, of course, unable for the moment to send him after us. So I began to explain matters about the Sunday Office in this wise:

The life of the Church, which is the soul of a Totum Breviary, begins with Easter. Now, Easter Sunday changes its date each year. It waits for the full moon of the spring equinox to give notice that it is time to start. This occurs always between the twenty-second of March and the twenty-fifth of April. From Easter Sunday we count fifty days, so that the seventh Sunday following is Pentecost Sunday. Then the number of weeks to Advent, which always precedes Christmas by four Sundays, may be twenty-four or more, since Easter occurs sometimes earlier and sometimes later, though always between the twenty-second of March and the twenty-fifth of April. If there are more than twenty-four Sundays from Pentecost to Advent, the liturgical Offices for these additional Sundays are supplied from the Offices after the Epiphany, since in that case the period between the Epiphany and Lent has been shortened by the earlier occurrence of Easter. Accordingly, when we have come to the twenty-third Sunday after Pentecost, and Advent has not yet arrived, we insert one or more of the Sundays from the Offices after the Epiphany, to fill the gap as needed for the Pentecost cycle.

Christmas, with its preparation of Advent (four weeks, though the fourth week may not be complete), has for more than a thousand years been dated on the twenty-fifth of December. The Epiphany follows on the sixth of January. But the next cycle has for its center the feast of Easter, with its remote preparation from Septuagesima and its introduction through Lent. If Easter occurs in March, the Epiphany cycle is shortened, and the omitted Sunday Offices furnish, as already stated, material for supplementing the Sunday service between the twenty-third and the last (called twenty-fourth) Sunday after Pentecost.

As I give the days on which Easter occurs in my Kalendarium, together with a "Tabula Paschalis nova reformata" and the movable feasts for years ahead, the Padre was able to count up the matter. He sighed when he was through with his calculations; but it taught him a lesson; and I think he will be his own orderly or Ordo-maker later on, when he gets used to my superior ways, though they are a little laborious; but *per ardua ad astra*.

II. A Point of Regularity in the Life of the Totum

The new moon of the vernal equinox, which means the point of springtime when the sun crosses the celestial equator, making the day and night equal in duration, gives us the signal for the movable feasts beginning with Easter Sunday. This is followed by the Ascension, Pentecost, Corpus Christi, and the other Sundays down to Advent. The order does not, however, interfere with the steady cycle of immovable feasts which record the life of Christ and His saints. That life is introduced by the Precursor, St. John, who leads us, through Advent, to the Nativity of Our Lord at Christmas. St. Luke describes it in his Gospel narrative. It is a beautiful picture which he painted for the converts from paganism, who knew as yet nothing about the Messias.

After the Nativity at Bethlehem and the Epiphany, when the Kings from the East started their procession, there follows a train of saints from the first of January to the end of the year, each having his or her fixed birthday, independently of the movable feasts. As a Totum, it is my office to inform clerics about these saints, just as I do about the great events of Our Lord's life. I din it into their heads and hearts every day, so that as they grow older they too may become saints and get into my calendar. But I do it in a brief way because, though they themselves often preach long sermons, they have the Bollandists, and Alban Butler, and others who explain the details; whereas, a Breviary must say things in a brief and pointed fashion. I can only take an hour or so of the average missionary priest's time each day, so as to give them opportunity to practice what I preach and to bring it to their flocks in the church, school, and especially on sick-calls.

III. THE PADRE STUDIES THE CALENDAR

The Padre looked at the time table and then grumbled, "Still an hour," which meant, as I found out, that in another hour we should get home—his and my future home. Though curious enough about the new place, I remained very quiet because the Father, while not praying, kept a close eye on me. He was little concerned with my insides and feelings, but was examining my uniform. I do not mean the overcoat (which here they call 'binding'), nor the overalls of black made by the nun of the convent from which we had just come. What seemed to engage his attention was the front, under my vest—the rabbi and Roman collar, so to speak, which I call "De Anno et ejus partibus." He was evidently somewhat disturbed (despite his learning in liturgical matters) about the *Epacts,* and *Dominical* and *Golden Letters*—Cyclus Epactarum, Litteras Dominicales, Litteræ Aureæ. There was a certain satisfaction, however, in instructing the Padre. He wanted to know matters from the bottom up—always. So I kept on telling him some things which, of course, he knew already. *Repetita juvant.*

There are twelve months in the year, and that makes fifty-two weeks or three hundred and sixty-five days, and nearly six hours, during which the sun travels through the zodiac. After four years those six hours, over the three hundred and sixty-five days, make up, as everybody can see, an additional day of twenty-four hours. That day is tacked on at the end of February, in what the Americans, who for the most part speak English, call "Leap Year." We say "Bissextilis"; that is, a year when the

68 AUTOBIOGRAPHY OF AN OLD BREVIARY

sixth day before the Calends of March was reckoned double.

I said "nearly six hours" to be accurate, since some seconds are wanting, which, when they amount to a full day, must be made up. Hence, Pope Gregory XIII, who governed the Church not long after Luther had been causing trouble with his mis-called reformation business, tried to bring some order into the habits of people by arranging a proper calendar. The calendar which we had up to that time was, like the Greek and Latin poems of the Humanists—Erasmus and his ilk—a relic which had been borrowed from the pagans, and was rather confusing. A clever Roman general, Julius Caesar, who aspired to the papacy some fifty years before Our Lord established it, tried to exercise the function of Sovereign Pontiff—Pontifex Maximus—and began by making a calendar. It did not satisfy people for any length of time.

Meanwhile the Church had been established but, being persecuted, she was unable to attend to the calendar. When eventually the real Popes were permitted to have their say to the world at large, matters were somewhat mixed up. Even the great Gregory I, who had organized the liturgical functions and the chant in the Church, must have been handicapped, if he was not napping, because in his "Responsoriale" he never mentions the Circumcision or Ash Wednesday, though he has Christmas all right on the twenty-fifth of December. He also gives the feast of the Chair of St. Peter correctly on the twenty-second of February, which is not surprising, seeing that he sat upon it.

After a while came the other Gregory, the thirteenth, who took things in hand. First he reorganized the methods of canon law and the systematic study of theology. For this purpose he called the most learned men

THE PADRE AND THE CALENDAR

of Europe to Borne. He opened at least six national colleges in the Holy City—for he liked smart people and was particularly fond of the Irish and the Germans. In fact, he found out for himself what was going on in the much-maligned states of Central Europe by having nunciatures in Vienna, Cologne and even Lucerne. In his discussion with the scholarly men around him, he discovered that we were all at sixes and sevens with the sun and the moon, though these were the celestial bodies set by God in the sky to regulate our days and nights. The world was actually ten days behind in its calculations with heaven. So Gregory sent out a Bull ordering that after the feast of St. Francis of Assisi, the fourth of October, we should all, on waking up on the following day, count it as the fifteenth of October—just as if we had been asleep for ten days. And so it happened. The Franciscans had talk at supper that evening, and when they woke up for Matins, the Friar Lector read from the new Martyrology about St. Fortunatus on the Aurelian Way, and three hundred martyrs of Cologne, and St. Hedwigis, but never a word about the whole group of saints, including two popes, St. Mark and St. Callistus, and St. Denis the Areopagite, whose feasts had occurred during the ten days that had been skipped.

So they set to work quickly making more saints, and a few years later sent P. Felix Cantalicius and P. Pascal Baylon straight to heaven, though without giving them at once their canonization papers. It stirred the other Orders also to make more saints. The Jesuits had already despatched their holy Founder, and Francis Borgia, and Francis Xavier, to engage tickets for Paradise, and young Stanislaus of Kostka was blessing the cradle of Aloysius Gonzaga to hail him as a companion saint twenty-three years later. Friar Thomas of Villanova also had earned his crown by observance of the Augustinian Rule, and as bishop and "Father of the Poor." So had Peter of Alcantara and John of Avila, leaving behind them the odor of sanctity, and inviting and attracting those who were still living to follow and swell the lists of my calendar. Meanwhile there was Cardinal Charles Borromeo among the seculars, still busy at Milan, though soon to go Home; and dear Teresa, working at Lisbon, who was to take St. Hedwigis' place on 15 October and make the Queen of Poland move up to 17 October.

IV. How Pope St. Gregory the Great Fixed the Sun-dial

As I was saying, Pope Gregory sent out a Bull ordering everybody to drop ten days which the calendar makers had added to the age of the world, as if Almighty God had not done rightly His own business, Everybody that knew anything about astronomy saw, of course, at once that the Pope was right; only the Russians did not; and it took Englishmen about a hundred and seventy years to see it, although it was no joke. So since 1752 the Britishers have conformed to our way in reckoning time; but their stubbornness dissatisfied the Americans, and hence they soon after declared their independence, accepting of course my calendar, with the arrangement for future calculation that had been made by Pope Gregory XIII.

To avoid trouble as far as possible hereafter, Pope Gregory laid down the rule that, whilst the year according to the common reckoning has three hundred and sixty-five days, all those years whose numbers are divisible by four hundred, and those divisible by four, but not by one hundred, shall have three hundred and sixty-six days. Thus it comes about that, beginning with 1700, three out of every four centesimal leap years—that is, 1700, 1800, 1900 (not, however, 2000) — should have three hundred and sixty-five days in our calendar reckoning.

V. The Golden Number, and What Comes of It

What puzzled the Father was much more, I think, the Golden Number, and the Dominical Letter, and the Epacts. So I shall have to tell him.

The Golden Number is a figure—between one and nineteen—which was regularly printed in golden letters upon old-fashioned Almanacs, to indicate the current year of the lunar cycle. The lunar cycle is a period of nineteen years by which the time of Easter, the first Sunday after the full moon of the-spring equinox, is calculated. The moon is a bit fickle in its movements, and so it happens that it gets out of harmony with the movements of the more steady sun. To make them agree at the end of the year (to adjust the solar and lunar years, as scientists would say), the Greek astronomer Meton had long ago (430 B.C.) invented a method. He had watched the moon and the sun, and found that the twelve lunations, or monthly periods into which we divide our years, fall short of the solar year by about eleven days. Every change in the moon, in any year, will accordingly occur eleven days earlier than it did the preceding year. But at the expiration of nineteen years they occur again nearly at the same time. Thus tally was kept on the unsteadiness of the moon, so that its being full at a given time could be computed in advance. Then we should know when to look for Easter.

A further help to accuracy in determining the days of

the solar (civil) month, on which the new and full moons occur, is the calculation of the monthly Epact. The word "Epact" is Greek and means "thrown in," to designate the days thrown in to make up the difference in duration between the lunar and solar years. These Epact days give us the age of the moon on each New Year's day. As I said above, the lunar year falls short of the solar year about eleven days. If the new moon of the lunar cycle falls on 1 January, the Epact is O. The following year the Epact of addition made to the lunar year is XI; in the third year it will be XXII. The Epact of the fourth year would be XXXIII; but on the thirtieth of these thirty-three days a new moon has again appeared, so that the Epact corresponding to the fourth year in the lunar cycle is III (the Golden Number).

The lunar month, you see, consists of twenty-nine days, eleven hours, forty-four minutes. Hence the monthly Epact or addition in January, which has thirty-one days according to our civil reckoning, is one day and six minutes. The Epact increases of course each month; and by December it reaches eleven days. If the lunar months are reckoned alternately at twenty-nine and thirty days the process of calculation is somewhat shortened. By subtracting the annual Epact from thirty-one we get the day on which the new moon of January falls. For February the new moon falls thirty days later; for March twenty-nine days later; for April thirty days later, and so on with the remaining months.

A further aid in determining the date of Easter, which always is a Sunday, is the Dominical Letter. It is one of the first seven letters of our alphabet indicating the relation of the Sundays to the year—to let us know on what date of January falls the first Sunday of that month in any given year. The year (1 January) always begins with the letter A. If that day is a Thursday, the following Sunday is marked D. Ordinarily the Dominical Letter would repeat itself every seventh year. But as a day is added to our Leap Year, and that day repeats the Letter of the normal day, we get *two* Dominical Letters for every Leap Year. Since this intercalation interrupts the sequence of the Dominical Letters seven times in twenty-eight years, the same order of Dominical Letters cannot recur oftener than once in twenty-eight years. Allowance must further be made for the first year of the century years which are calculated as Leap Years.

The baggage delivery man is going through the train, and the Padre interrupted his attention to me by giving him directions for the express agent about his trunk. I shall have to hurry up a bit with my explanation.

I saw that my master wanted to know how one could remember the Dominical Letters for all the months of the year, so as more readily to count up the Sundays. Happily I could recall a distich made by a clever monk; though I don't allow it to get into my Totum, because that kind of poetry smacks a bit of the pagan classics. Here it is:

Astra Dabit Dominus—*Gratisque Beabit Egenos.*
Gratia Christiocolæ Feret Aurea Dona Fideli.

This couplet of verses by the initials of the words shows that A is the letter for January, D for February and again for March, and so on. But let me give an illustration to make the matter practical, though it demands of course some brains and attention to understand it all. Suppose you want to know on what day Easter Sunday fell in 1879.

Our Lord was born, according to the common reckoning, at the end of the first year in the lunar cycle.

So we add *one* to the year in question—1879, which makes 1880. Divide this number by nineteen, which is the number of years it takes the moon to get steady and come back to the same place, nearly.

$$\frac{1880}{19} = 98, \text{ leaving a remainder of } 18,$$

which is the Golden Number corresponding to the Epact VII in my calendar. This means that January 1, 1879, the moon was seven days old, or rather had started on its regular tramp seven days before. By subtracting seven from thirty-one we ascertain that the new moon is due again on 24 January, and on 21 February and on 24 March, getting full for the Easter celebration fifteen days later, when the spring equinox occurs (8 April). The Sunday following will be Easter. To make sure on what day of the week 8 April falls, we need the Dominical Letter. In my table you notice it is E, and if you remember the old monk's verses you will see how it comes about. April has the indication G, then comes A for 2 April, B for 3 April. The Dominical Letter E comes on 6 April, which therefore must have been a Sunday. The next Sunday is 13 April—Easter Sunday. *Capite?*

Here the Padre hustled me into his grip, and we had to get out. It was rather dark and I feared we should get lost, though I was not allowed much light anyway, and had to put up with a corner, resting on an old nightshirt—a most undignified position for me. From the jolting I judged that we had hired a cab and were at length at the end of our journey.

Per varios casus et tot discrimina rerum, as my friend, St. Jerome, used to quote from some Roman pagan poet. That was before his conversion, and after he had read some of the Bible and received Baptism as a real

Christian from Pope Liberius.

I was getting a little restless with this continuous irregularity of traveling, and of meeting all sorts of distracting things and people. But then I had the satisfaction of having taught the Padre a thing or two, which not everybody knows or even can understand. He is likely, too, to spread the benefit to others, probably to young clerics, and later on to priests, who can do much good by their regular and holy lives if they practice what I preach to them every day for over an hour. I wonder if the Padre will introduce me to them in his Liturgy class. He is very good company, of course, by himself; but then I should like to be an assistant professor also. However, I must keep quiet, for if he heard me he would say: "You want the earth," which is true enough, because I am a B. R. Totum.

Third Part

I. AT HOME AND IN THE SEMINARY

AT LAST we are at home and settled, I have no vocation to be a Friar or companion to a missionary who wanders from place to place. For a Totum it would be undignified to be running about. Besides, I am a bit stout by nature, and if I got into a perspiration it might ruin my complexion and health. The Padre would lose all respect for me; and if there is one thing which I feel in duty bound to assert at all times, it is my native gravity.

Here everything is in good order. In fact, I never expected such considerate treatment as I am getting in this new world. Where I was born they talk about the American Indians with their tomahawks, about the Wild West, and the uncultivated prairie lands of the United States. There is nothing here of that kind. I don't believe Belgium or France has quarters like this for anybody but bishops and cardinals. The sitting-room of the Padre, who is just a simple priest, though a professor, has a red velvet couch entirely for me; that is to say, I am on top of it. I have the prie-dieu, with a shelf on the second floor, to myself, except when the Padre puts his elbows on it; and that is never for very long. In fact, he prefers to say his prayers kneeling on the wooden floor. Whenever he comes for me, he just for a minute puts his arms on my cushions to help recollection. Then he rises and respectfully lifts me up also. With his mind on me, the Totum, thus elevated he walks about, pretty much as Enoch did in God's company.

Whilst I used to lie there on the sumptuous prayer-stool, I could see and hear things which sharpened my observation. Soon after the Padre had emptied his valise on our arrival here, the disreputable company with which I had to associate on the journey, was put in its proper place. There were receptacles for everything—a pipe-stand, the wash-basket, a low rack for pamphlets, and a whole row of bookshelves around the walls. It was quite a respectable company of volumes.

Some people made an awful noise about the place when we first came in, though at the time I could see nothing, being in the bag. There must have been a sort of reception, and one could hear music, and the talk of men, in a more or less indistinct way. They all seemed to like the Padre, for one can tell from the high key of voices when there is joy in human noises. On the whole, I don't think I missed much. I have learnt since then (from corners at the sideboards in dining-halls and sundry other places) that there is a good deal of "vox et præterea nihil" at these receptions. Even priests like a little taffy occasionally, and when they talk in the presence of higher dignitaries you can hardly believe a word they say, though they are truthful enough at other times. I suppose it is the fashion all the world over, and will in some way be straightened out, when men get their passports to heaven with a visa on the back, recommending a strong Turkish bath, before admitting them to paradise.

When the Padre had at last got into his room, the first night after our arrival, and thought about recovering from the big supper they had inflicted upon him, though he never said anything about it, there came a knock, and a servant looked in with: "Doctor, your trunk has just come. Shall I bring it up here?" Good Lord, they call the

Padre "Doctor" here. I knew he had been "Monsieur le Professeur," but now he comes with a new title. Among my intimate acquaintances and closer friends are the great Doctors Ambrose, Augustine, Jerome and Gregory. They are solid saints. Then after-ward I got to know closely St. Thomas, whom Pope Pius V introduced to me. Later Pope Sixtus V brought in St. Bonaventure. Then gradually other Doctors got the entree—St. Bernard, St. Hilary, St. Alphonsus, St. Francis de Sales; even St. Cyril of Alexandria, though a foreigner, came to stay with me, for he knew our language and manners, as did St. John Damascene. Finally we invited to our roundtable the true English gentleman St. Bede, and just now there is a waiting list. But these have all had a formal introduction as canonized saints. Hence, I shall not commit myself, much as I esteem the Padre, nor call him "Doctor," until he is presented in regular form by card on my calendar.

To my astonishment I saw, when the Padre opened his trunk, that he took out a Totum just like myself. I knew it the moment I saw the brown wrapper, such as I had worn while we all were waiting for appointments in the upper story at Tournai. This was evidently an interference, and I could hardly suppress a pang of jealousy at the suspicion that here was a cousin of my own, who, if he gained the Padre's affection, was sure to poach on my preserves. I did not know what were the parish regulations in America; but the thought that it was a free country, and that perhaps the Canon Law about permission to exercise jurisdiction in another parish was not sufficiently known, began to worry me a bit. However, I kept perfectly quiet on my prie-dieu, though the reflection made me, I think, blush a bit. Besides, I did not want those old crozier heads on the shelf under me to think I was excited. One has to keep up a certain reserve before inferiors. Well, I might have known better than to suspect that anyone could alienate the affections of the Padre from me, after the services by which I had proved my attachment to him during the last few weeks, when the other Totum must have been sleeping in the hold of the vessel, and later associating with low folk generally in the freight department and baggage cars. My master looked at the imported stowaway and then put him quietly in a drawer, which was as good as being "on the shelf."

II. The Padre Takes the Totum to School

During the next few days we kept up our usual conversations, and if there had been any suspicion of misunderstanding, it was all made up between us.

One Friday morning the Padre came into the room with a lot of notes, and seemed a bit fussy when he heard a bell ringing. I had noticed that bell soon after we had first entered the house. It was too regular to be a fire bell, and it could not have been a Mass bell because it rang at all hours, morning and evening, starting as early as five o'clock A. M. I soon got used to it and asked no questions.

Evidently there was something wrong with the Padre. He unceremoniously picked me up and put me under his arm. As he had said Little Hours immediately after Mass, and I know we could not say Vespers now—at least we had never done it in the forenoon—the action completely upset me. To be carried under one's arm like an ordinary school book was, to say the least, unusual in my case. My astonishment grew when we marched into a large hall with a row of benches occupied by shaven young men who looked for all the world like imitations

THE TOTUM AT SCHOOL 81

of priests. Some of them even had on Roman collars. It dawned on me that this might be a choir service because, among the regulations which I always carry with me to guide me in my conduct amidst the clergy, there are some that refer to "In Choro." I had not hitherto paid much attention to these regulations, for they seem to me reserved for special occasions, like parliamentary rules or the ceremonies to be observed at court functions. But these fresh-looking youths were evidently much below the Professor and myself in rank; and I saw at once, when we took the raised seat fronting the assembly, that we were going to teach them manners, with me for model. And so it was.

The first thing, after saying a short prayer to the Holy Ghost, with the added invocation "Sedes Sapientias, ora pro nobis," the Padre delivered a sort of academic speech. It was about the importance of theological study, and ended in a eulogy of your humble Totum. It almost brought a blush from under my gilt edges, but I managed to keep a dignified silence in front of him. On principle I am opposed to flattery of myself, even if it come from one as sincere and truthful as the Padre. Hence I shall not repeat all that he said in my praise. Later he became more didactic, and announced that he would first speak to them of the importance of reverent attention in reciting the Breviary. This reverent attention, he said, depends almost entirely upon a proper understanding of the purpose, structure, and correct practice of the Divine Office as embodied in the Breviary.

III. He Draws a Picture of Titynillus and His Wicked Ways

At the end of this introductory speech, which lasted about an hour, the Padre made a bow and went out amid the silence of the young clerics. As I gleaned from the address, they were all theologians who had already made a partial course in Dogma, Moral and Liturgy. Now that I had been introduced, they all brought out Roman Breviaries, which claimed to be relations of mine; but none of them was anything to boast of. I recognized certain family traits, which was easy enough, considering my ancient pedigree. Most of them were poor, a thing I should not have minded if they had had the character of a Totum, with my recognized consistency and gravity of deportment. Instead of that, they were mostly half-grown and puny-looking, with half pagan names like "Pars Hiemalis," "Pars Autumnalis," "Pars Verna," and "Pars Æstiva," which also showed that they were afraid of the weather at certain seasons of the year and could not be seen in the open at all times, like myself.

The next time the Padre went into that room with me, he spoke of the "Aperi Domine." This prayer, he said, corresponded to the ablutions which the Jews were commanded to make before beginning their solemn offices as levites and priests.[4] Of course, it is to be understood in a moral or spiritual sense, as when St. Paul speaks of Christ's word being the water that cleanses the Church and thereby sanctifies it.[5] The Professor paid a tribute to my eloquence and holiness in general when he said that I was not to be talked to without their

---

[4] See Exod. 29:4, and again 30:18-31; 40: 7, 20-22; also Num. 8:7 etc.

[5] Ephes, 5: 26 and Hebr. 10:22.

remembering my dignity. If they wished to get an audience with His Divine Majesty through me, who am the official messenger of the Church and the faithful, they should pay attention to what I said—*attente*. I would talk to them of God, which had to be done—*digne*. Next we were to pray together some part of the time each day. Accordingly, they were to keep head and heart piously bent—*devote*. In short, they must attend to their business with me well—*bene dicendum*; and, dismissing all sorts of vain, trifling and perverse thoughts and preoccupations, attend to the one thing—*hoc Officium.*

He brought home his point by drawing a picture of the devil, whom he called "Tytinillus," wherever he got the name. This archfiend, he said, was sure to follow stealthily after a cleric, and watch him during the recitation of the Divine Office. It was almost amusing the way he described Satan coming along on crutches, with a basket on his ugly shoulders, and picking up every mispronounced word and every syllable slurred over. He maintained that the devil collected all the voluntary distractions and interruptions, and put them in his *"sportella"* to be presented on judgment day by the "advocatus diabolus," and that he was sure to harass the poor dying priest in his last hours, by way of temptation to despair, for having done his Master's work negligently, and for having failed to obtain for the faithful what he was deputed to pray for in the daily repetition of the Office. Then, to illustrate his point further, he recited to them a sort of poem like a hymn, though it could not of course come up to the poetry and grace of what is found in a Totum. Still, they all copied the verses. I remember them, though I would not allow them into my parlor. Here they are—a kind of admonitory medieval Latin jingle:

Canonicas Horas
Si devote legis, oras.
Tunc orantur Horas
Si corde leguntur et ore.
Litera neglecta
Vel syllaba
murmure tecta
Colligit hæc Satana
Dum non cum corde laboras.
Fragmina verborum
Tytinillus colligit horum,
Quaque die mille Vicibus sarcinat ille.

Cur induis acta vagorum
Qui debitor officiorum
Es divinorum?
Desine vagari foras
Nam Christus ponderat horas,
Et notando moras
Distinguit qualiter oras.
Qui psalmos resecat
Et verba Davidica curtat,
Displicet ille Deo
Dum placuisse putat.

Cum Deum pie invocas
Psallendo teipsum honoras.
Dirige cor sursum,
Attente profer discursum.
Nunc lege, nunc ora,
Et sic cum Petro labora.

IV. The Traveling Cleric

I thought the Padre would begin today by giving my family history and pedigree, which is very important. But he went back to discourse about the necessity of getting a clear notion and conviction regarding the reverent treatment of the Divine Office. He talked more like an apostle than like a professor, and came pretty near making me think that many priests did not know what they were doing when they went to recite their Breviary. I had not, it is true, a very large experience. But even during the few days in the seminary, I had seen several visiting clerics saying their Office; they made me doubt that they had actually been ordained, though they were in Roman collar and black garb, and the students called them "Father." One came near borrowing me from the prie-dieu, while waiting for the Padre in his room one afternoon. But just as he was going to introduce himself to me, in came the Padre. Afterward both of them went out on the seminary green, and I went along.

When they had finished their talk, the visitor looked at his watch and said: "I have half an hour before my train starts. I guess I can finish Little Hours meanwhile, but I'll have to go and borrow a Breviary." The Padre said nothing, because he and I had to have our Matin chat about that time. The visitor, who seemed to be quite at home in the place, came back with another young priest. The latter carried a set of tools, with which he was going to construct a sun-dial. They both nodded to the Professor, and whilst the one began to measure something, the other walked along and began "Jam lucis orto sidere, Deum precemur supplices, ut in diurnis actibus nos servet a nocentibus." I thought it strange, because the day was nearly gone and his prayer could hardly avail him much. After a while he stopped to see how the sun-dial was getting on, and then went to a seat nearby. But he was restless and reminded me of a hen that looks for a place to lay her egg in. All the while the Padre was talking to me quietly, and I wondered at the way he minded his business. All at once the guest jumped up shouting: "Good Lord, I shall miss my train," and adding, "Good-by, Professor; good-by, John," ran off, leaving the Breviary irreverently on the unused dog-kennel at the gate as he went out. He could hardly have got to the middle of Terce. Perhaps the Padre had this case in mind when he pointed out to the young theologians what hindered a cleric chiefly from reciting his Breviary "digne, attente ac devote."

V. THE PADRE BECOMES CRITICAL.

"When you begin your Office," the Padre said, "look for a moment up at the crucifix on the wall. Note the five wounds upon the extended, all-embracing figure of our Master. They are in part the result of five slashings which a cleric inflicts while badly performing the duty of the Canonical Hours." Faults and defects of this kind, he said, are almost habitual. They are the result of untrained or unrestrained temperament. He gave five different names to those whom he thus characterized among the clergy.

The clerical *Prayer-machine*—that is, a cleric who recites his Office daily in a mechanical and perfunctory way. It is all said—but without thought and without the prayerful sense which is its essential strength and life. The habit comes with those mostly who are constitutionally light-headed. These men never make a serious meditation; they act, as a rule, like a watch wound up to run down and point the time. Such clerics lack serious aims in life; they are the sort of men who say conventional things; they are nice, but give no actual help to the Church.

The clerical *Flywheel*—that is, a cleric who recites with feverish haste, to get through a job. He may appreciate the thought and know the beauty of the Divine Office, but he does not give himself time to drink it in and profit by it so as to feed his spiritual or pastoral life. That too is often the result of constitutional habit. But this fact does not lessen the irreverence with which haste treats the sacred deposit intended for the purpose of arousing reflection and thereby enriching the priestly life-blood.

The *Tyrian* cleric. I should hardly have known what sort of priest he meant, thinking at first that the name referred to some new Religious Order; but he explained that it was suggested by the words of the prophet Ezechiel who in chapter twenty-seven speaks of the Tyrians engrossed in secular affairs, the pursuit of business and magnificently successful, yet so as to forget the ordinances of God and thereby come to grief.

The next species he called clerical *Weathervanes.*—By this name he designated the superficial cleric who turns, as it were, on a pivot, and is ready to change with every breath of air around him. He is alive to all sorts of pleasantries, interrupting the Office on the slightest pretext, so that no one would believe he was doing any serious reading, much less praying.

Finally, the Padre spoke of the shepherds of souls, who, whilst ostensibly representing the watches on the walls and towers of the Church, are asleep. These he called the *Nightcaps.* The name seemed hardly consistent and had nothing to do with drinks; but was meant to indicate the class of clerics who habitually put off the recitation of the Office to the last minute; as if everything else were of greater importance. Some say that this is no fault, because the Lord is patient. But, as the Padre explained, it is a grievous wrong to bank on that patience knowingly. It is almost a sin against the Holy Ghost.

It was surprising what hard things the Professor said about these five variations of "professional" apostles, as he called them. But then he was, of course, talking only about states and conditions that were not supposed to exist, in the minds of the students. He merely wanted to frighten them away from the actual neglect of what was really a wonderful arrangement of Divine Providence to preserve the future shepherds of souls from deteriorating into a set of hirelings. If they became prayer-machines, such as the Chinese employ in their pagodas, that is, just wheels turned by a person to rattle off a certain number of invocations, they had no right or title to ordination. He said they were or would be just "shams," like quacks, not to be tolerated in any profession, since they not only pretended to do what they did not perform rightly, but proclaimed themselves to be what they were not. Christ called them whited sepulchers, for they made pretensions to a living that they did not earn, to honors and to promotions that gave them titles which they discredited. They were untrustworthy for they broke their promises made at ordination, and violated the pledges under which they were admitted to the priesthood.

It was pretty hard to listen to him, especially for one who knew the Padre, as I did, for a mild and charitable person. But he wound up all right; he exhorted them with what came near being a sermon, though we were in a class-hall. I heard the students afterward commenting on it. Some of them had higher ideals than others; but they all realized that to treat the Breviary, which included my poor relations, with disrespect or neglect, implied low views of the spiritual life, a certain degree of professional dishonesty, and a niggardliness by giving to God and the Church a secondary and slovenly treatment which they would not give to men and institutions which they professed to respect. It all speaks well for the dignity of the Totum.

Fourth Part

I. The Noble Pedigree of the Totum

TODAY the Padre did me great honor. He told the young theologians that the Breviary—he meant of course the Totum—belonged in fact to the old nobility of the *Ordo Missæ*. That Order antedates the *flaiths,* or aristocracy, of Patrician Ireland, which outranks the knighted heroes of the Crusades and of the French Legion of Honor. In the primitive Church the Breviary actually performed the office of *major-domo,* introducing to the assembly of the faithful the Pontiff who was to celebrate the Holy Sacrifice and bring down from heaven the Son of the Most High King.

The liturgical worship at first was formulated and ordered by the apostles. They received their instructions during the Forty Days after the Resurrection, when Our Lord was with them, to the day of His Ascension, on Mount Olivet; and the ordinations were completed shortly afterward on the feast of Pentecost. The exercises thus approved consisted, for the greater part, of the recitation of the Psalter, with which the Jewish converts were already familiar. The psalms, recalling the story of God's mercies to His chosen people, were interspersed with readings from the Prophets, foretelling the Messianic advent. All of this served as a prelude to the sublime act of "The Breaking of Bread." It was the duty of the Totum— one of my relations still quite young at that time —to accompany the Vicar of Christ in the daily worship, and to usher in the Lord of Hosts with song and prayer.

Admission to these exercises was reserved. The new converts from Judaism or paganism, who were being instructed in the Faith of Christ and His Church, but who had not yet been baptized, were allowed to take part only in the preliminary acts of prayer. But when it came to the actual Offering of the Holy Sacrifice, they were told publicly by a deacon that they must leave the assembly. Then the bishop began the Secret, preceding the holy mysteries of solemn Consecration, at which all the priests assisted in the sanctuary, and the baptized and reconciled faithful attended in the body of the church. Here too the Totum sometimes took part in the processional devotions which accompanied the Mass on special occasions, such as the days which in later times became the solemn feasts of Corpus Christi, or Candlemas, or during Holy Week.

Then came a time, after Constantine's day, when the newly-ordained bishops and presbyters were kept busy preaching and organizing parishes everywhere, and when the faithful, growing in numbers, were no longer obliged to resort to the catacombs or private places of worship. They could attend Mass and instruction, and after that go about their accustomed duties without risk of life or apprehension of sudden martyrdom. As a result the liturgical services were shortened, and those whose inclination or leisure permitted them to attend special prayers and acts of devotion, gathered for the purpose, at different hours and in separate places. Thus the chanting and recitation of psalms and lessons, with antiphons and responsories, which hitherto had been performed by all in common who were present at the *Introit* or introductory services of the Mass, became a distinct practice. It was separated from the Oblation, Consecration, and Communion, and took on the character of a canonical office performed at fixed hours before Mass.

Then the Pope desired to have the Totum revised, and St. Jerome got orders to do it. He did it to suit the Roman clergy; but somehow it was a misfit. Later he tried it again; and the new suit was much better and was approved by the French bishops when they came to Rome to have their liturgical measure taken by the Sovereign Pontiff, the *Forma gregis Christi*. That is how I got the name of having a new suit from France (Gallican Psalter, they called it). They made new rubrics telling how to wear it at the daily attendance in the churches where there could be no interference with the Pontifical Mass.

As the celebrant could not do entirely without my assistance, he borrowed my short psalms and antiphons, and made an *Introit* of it for the Mass. This was to be recited before the Offeratory, on the steps of the altar.

In such way I, the Totum, had a place assigned all to myself, of course in the sanctuary. Here the clergy met at stated hours, both before the solemn Mass and after it, following my directions for chanting the *Horæ Canonicæ*. They were not simply saying their prayers or accompanying the liturgical services. No, the Vicar of Christ ordered that they were to chant the *Horæ* in solemn unison in the name of the entire Church; that is to say, for the faithful all the world over.

It is wonderful, to think that the Totum was not simply to be a collection of prayers and devout readings, as it had been handed down from the Jewish Synagogue, to express the devotion of the attending congregation. No, it was to be the voice of the High Priest on earth calling to God in the name of the whole world, *Urbis et Orbis*, for mercy, and in thanksgiving. Soon I was in demand everywhere. The anchorites and hermits also in the desert copied me. They carried my likeness into all parts of the world, even where they could not celebrate the Holy Sacrifice of the Mass. Then St. Benedict came and organized regular choirs of monks, who alternately chanted the divine praises from the Totum, night and day. Oh, it was glorious to hear the voices rise to heaven in the solitudes of the Libyan plains and in the forests of Lombardy, just the same as they did in the grand basilicas which had been built by the Roman emperor, Constantine!

Sometimes it happened that the members of the monasteries were separated from the Community. Even then the individuals kept up the practice of following my regulations. They would, though alone, repeat the responses and antiphons as well as the chapters. They would say "Jube, Domine, benedicere" or "Benedicite" and "Dominus vobiscum" just as if the abbot and the brethren were all there; for they knew they spoke and prayed in the name of the whole Church. In this way the Office of the Totum served as a preparation and a thanksgiving in connection with the Mass celebrated everywhere from the rising to the setting of the sun.

One of the Irish students seemed to think I was indebted for my Gallican excellencies rather to St. Patrick and St. Columbanus than to St. Gregory of Tours, who, the Padre had said, was the first to bring me from Rome to France. This new seminarian continually asked questions in class. Today he wanted to know whether the Antiphonary of Bangor (the boy was from Carrickfergus) was not the original of the Gallican Psalter. He had before him a volume of Archdall-Moran and quoted from it, translating the Irish:

> Excellent the rule of Bangor.

> Correct and divine,
> Exact, holy, constant,
> Exalted, just and admirable.

He maintained that King Cormack and Columbanus himself used to recite the Breviary psalms, which were different from those of the Roman Psalter; and that could only have been what they call the Gallican Psalter, the same that is in the Breviary now. He thought that it was time the Irish came into their rights in matters of liturgy as much as in politics.

Of course, I knew all along that the student was wrong. But whether the Padre knew it or not, he did not enter into the question. He smiled simply, and said that the Breviary had a great ancestry, but that the details of its history would have to be discussed later. Their first object was to master the practical part that led to its understanding and to an intelligent recitation. But he insisted on reverence, and told them about the esteem in which the Totum was held during the Middle Ages, when not only priests and religious men and women in monasteries, but lay persons, and soldiers, like the Knights of the Holy Sepulcher, the Templars, the Militia of the Holy Ghost, nay even many of the various trade guilds, recited the psalms and prayers of the canonical Offices daily, amid all kinds 'of secular avocations. In that way the "Little Offices," and what were called breviaries, antiphonaries, and prayer chaplets, came into vogue. For a short time he dwelt on the beauty of my structure; he called it the anatomy of the Divine Office, which, he said, was simply perfect, like the conception of manly beauty such as the Greeks pictured to themselves under the image of Apollo; only that the Totum had also a beautiful soul—the soul of prayer.

It almost made me burst with pride when I remembered it all that evening, as the Padre took me into the chapel, where he often said his Matins and Lauds for the next day. I should have liked to see the picture of Apollo; but though there were some souvenirs of special patron saints put in my care—between the leaves—Apollo was not among them. Afterward I recalled that I had somewhere heard the name mentioned; I think, in an Epistle of St. Paul. It sounded a bit pagan, and so I put it out of my head.

What he meant, no doubt, was that the order and arrangement of parts in a Totum are perfect, not only from the devotional but from the esthetic or artistic point of view. This I was glad to know, because it is one thing to feel that one is good, and another to know that one is also beautiful. Both things redound to the glory of God; and the dignity and efficiency of a Totum as a guide for priests and bishops and as a fountain of wisdom and discipline are matters of importance. That was not, however, the sole reason for my elation. The fact that the Padre praised my beauty refutes the notion which some people entertain that the Roman Breviary lacks the polish and grace of classical diction. They allow that the Totum contains all that may be expected from a priests' prayer-book; yet they imagine that it is not enough to be devotional. They want you to be a classic, like Homer, or some of those old Greek or Roman pagans. But stop—

The Padre is thumping me on the sides as if to say: No vain thoughts, my Totum. "Munda cor meum ab omnibus vanis, perversis et alienis cogitationibus." So I must recollect myself and mind my P's and Q's.

II. The Ordinary of the Office

Next morning I was seriously scandalized. The Padre overslept. As a result he was late in the sacristy for Mass. I might not have noticed it but for the fact that I was actually neglected. Besides, the Father was led, I fear, through this, into a slight prevarication. After his Mass, that is to say, not until nearly eight o'clock, he took me up and began "Jam lucis orto sidere," which, if I know anything, means that the sun has just risen. Now, the official calendar states that the sun at this time of the year rises at 4:45 o'clock, or 4:48 to be precise. The professor of astronomy, who has some kind of queer instrument in his room, showed it on a dial exposed near the clock in the tower; and he is mighty particular. Only native respect kept me from reminding the Padre, when he said "Jam," that it was actually three hours since we should have had our talk at Prime and Terce.

But he seemed out of sorts or perhaps he was only sorry, for he hardly ate any breakfast. He had to come in late the night before, which is not very often his way. Like myself, he wants regularity, and especially a good sleep. We both have got a permit from the highest ecclesiastical authority to keep our Vigils in daytime—to anticipate them, as they say—and so we do; though the Professor wants a little nap after dinner, while I doze on the prie-dieu.

Later I found out what had been the trouble. The Padre had been beguiled into playing cards after the usual hour. He is not much good at it, and never puts his mind right down to it. He thinks that winning or losing is a matter of chance; and there is the temptation. For in those hazard games you have to play for stakes. They may not amount to much; but if you win you are bound to keep on, and if you lose you are also bound to keep on; since in either case they say you are not a good sport if you drop out. Whether the Padre lost or won I do not know, for he is very reticent in such matters and in general has not much to say about money. I doubt if he keeps what he gets, for when he goes out I often notice the tramps run after him. They mostly come away smiling. Still, if he begins to keep late hours, I fear me he will go to the "d. d. bowwows," as some literary genius whom they quote used to say.

Alas, it was all rash judgment on my part. The Padre does play cards, as he plays billiards or chess, though he is no expert at any of these things. But he believes that such games, moderately used, furnish means of promoting sociability, and that, if a man looks to self-improvement, he can find no better practical method than the restraints which properly regulated and temperate exercise imposes in the taking of recreation. The prejudice against card games is due to the want of moderation, that is to say, to the wild and prolonged betting to which it entices men who lack appreciation of the value of time or the will-power to control their enjoyment of a diversion.

The Examinations are on. For several days there has been apparently a good deal of worry, comparing notes and late clandestine keeping of lights in the rooms of senior class-members, poring over Hurter and Gury, Tanquerey and Konings, and other learned authors who try to explain away the simple truths which they could find in the Totum if only they used their brains properly. But today they made a great fuss about me. A number of the professors came in, to find out what the students in the last year of theology, who were to be promoted to Sacred Orders, knew about the Breviary.

I did not like it—I mean the Exam—for though I am pretty well accustomed to hear myself talked about, they did not treat me with the reverence which I experience every day at the hands of the Padre. They seemed to be merely curious about my insides, and asked me a lot of questions. For instance:

"What is the Ordinary of the Roman Breviary?"

The young cleric—he was somewhat nervous—answered well enough. He did not confine himself to the question proposed, but rattled off the whole set of my contents.

"The Ordinary," he said, "is that part of the daily Office which belongs to every feast and ferial throughout the year. It includes the

> Invitatory,
> Hymns,
> Psalms with their antiphons,
> Lessons with their responses, and
> Canticles."

The professor who was asking, evidently had his doubts about that answer; still, he seemed pleased with the assurance of the youth, who looked very prim and neatly groomed in his soutane and deep Roman collar.

III. THE INVITATORY

"And what do you mean by *Invitatory*?" he interrupted.

Invitatory means an invitation to pray, to recite the Office. It was at first simply a call issued in the morning at the hour of rising. In the Benedictine monasteries one of the monks would always have to be on watch. When it was time for the monks to get up for the morning prayer he would make the rounds from cell to cell, and knock, saying aloud:

'*Venite, exultemus Domino.*'

Then the monk in his cell would rise from his couch and say in answer, to show that he was awake:

'*Venite, adoremus.*' "

"And do you say *'Venite, exultemus Domino'* every morning," the examiner asked, "without exception throughout the year, when you begin your Breviary?"

"Yes, every day, though not necessarily in the morning. One could say it in the evening; that is, before a feast, because the ecclesiastical or liturgical day begins at sundown and ends at sundown."

"Indeed, so the *Venite, exultemus Domino* is just a monkish formula for rousing the brethren from sleep, which has been retained in the practice of the Church? There is a Lenten antiphon, if I remember rightly, which precedes the *Venite, exultemus,* and which seems to be a continuation of the Invitation. It runs like this: *Non sit vobis vanum mane surgere ante lucem, quia promisit Dominus coronam vigilantibus.* Is that correct?"

"Oh, no. The *Venite* is the ninety-fourth psalm of our Vulgate. It is preceded by an *antiphon* which is repeated after each couplet, and which varies with the liturgical seasons or with different feasts. But the psalm is always the same for the opening of the Matins."

"And what is this antiphon you speak of? Why would the same phrase be repeated so often, breaking up the continuity of the psalm? Once said, it ought to be enough, since Our Lord warns us not to make many words or repeat prayers like the heathens do."

"No, Sir. This repetition of prayer was a Divine ordinance given to the Hebrews, as we know from the Scriptures."

"Indeed—where? Can you give us an example and explain how it was used?"

"I only remember one instance definitely. It occurs in the *Hallel* Psalms, the one hundred thirty-fifth, in which each strophe—I think there are twenty-six—ends with the same refrain:

"*Quoniam in æternum misericordia ejus.*" The pilgrims to the temple at Jerusalem used to sing it like a litany, in which one who knew the Psalm by memory acted as a sort of chanter, and the rest of the pilgrims just repeated the refrain. In the early Church the people, many of whom could not read or had not books as we have them now, took part in the public prayers and chantings of the liturgy. One of the clerics would sing a short phrase easily remembered by the congregation and embodying the principal thought of the Psalm. The faithful would at once repeat the phrase in the same tone, again and again at intervals, when the sign was given by the antiphonarian. In this way they all took part in the service. Sometimes, as in the Invitatory, the chanter who presided would announce the feast of the day, and then intone a short phrase to that effect, to be repeated by the congregation. For example: *Deum unum in Trinitate Trinitatem in Unitate—venite adoremus*, for Trinity Sunday. In this way the faithful took active part in the liturgical prayers, especially the chanting of the Psalms. Thence are derived the antiphons:

> Regem Angelorum,
> Regem Apostolorum,
> Regem Martyrum,
> Regem Confessorum,
> Regem Virginum,

and so forth, with the addition, *Venite, adoremus.* When at times the services had to be shortened, they just repeated these invocations, or antiphons at the beginning and end of each psalm. Our present custom of antiphons, before and after the psalms, is a remnant of the ancient practice. Every priest repeats it, because, even in the private recitation of the Office, he represents the entire Church."

"That is very interesting," said the examining professor, "but tell me—do you always say the entire antiphon before and after each psalm? I think there are times—semi-double feasts, for instance—when we repeat only part of it, especially at the beginning. Is it not strange to be just chanting or reciting three or four words, often without any completed meaning, at the beginnings of the psalms?"

IV. Intoning the Antiphons

"The custom," replied the student, "of merely intoning the antiphons before the psalms was I believe, introduced later in the liturgy, when a distinction was made in the solemnity of feasts. Some feasts were celebrated by a full chanting of all the antiphons before and after the psalms. These were called feasts of double rite (*Duplex*). Other feasts of minor rite were indicated by just intoning the antiphon, that is, by chanting or reciting half of it, or the opening words. These were called semi-doubles. It was simply a method of announcing to the faithful present at the services, that the day was not a solemn but a simple feast or a ferial."

"Does not the term *antiphon* have a larger signification than that applied to the short phrases at the beginning and end of psalms, or (as in the case of the Invitatory at intervals in the midst of it?"

"Yes, Sir, it is used for what we call Verses and Responses, which have the same origin and purpose of making the faithful take part in the public prayer. The Verses and Responses are chanted separately; that is, independently of the psalms. They represent two alternate groups of the faithful charting the Divine praises in short phrases.

"The term *antiphon* is also applied to hymns or proses chanted by the entire congregation, because they are well known to all, and therefore readily taken up when intoned by the pre-chanter."

V. The Ninety-fourth Psalm

The professor seemed quite satisfied, on the whole, if one might judge from the way he smiled when he turned to the Father Rector saying: "I suppose that suffices."

But the Padre wanted to know more.

"I find here," he said, opening me, the Totum, "on the feast of the Epiphany, that there is no *Invitatorium*. Hence your definition of Ordinarium, and what you said of the daily repetition of the Invitatory is wrong. The Ninety-fourth Psalm is there in the Office of the

Epiphany, true enough, in the Third Nocturn. It is not, however, found there as the Invitatorium. In fact, there is none at all. Moreover, the text is slightly different. Not only is the Latin reading changed in parts, as for example:

> Et siccam manus ejus formaverunt
> Et aridam formaverunt manus ejus;

but there are omissions of passages like

> Quoniam non repellet Dominus plebem suam

and alterations like

> altitudines montium ipsius sunt

for

> altitudines montium ipse conspicit.

Will you tell me first why there is no Invitatory on the feast of the Epiphany, and, in the next place, why the Psalm is changed from the Vulgate text? This appears also to be a violation of the canons of the Council of Trent, which oblige us to use the Latin Version revised from the Hebrew by St. Jerome. The rule applies, I should think, to the Psalms as well as to other parts of the Bible for public use in church."

The little cleric wasn't stumped a bit. He waited for a minute and then said:

"Why, Sir, on the Epiphany there is no need of an Invitatory. It used to be on the festival day for Christmas when everybody was expected to keep awake, because it was Holy Night. The Christians kept vigil with the Magi who came, guided by the light of a blazing star. The omission of the Invitatory on the Epiphany is symbolical of the watch which the kings as well as the shepherds observed at the birth of Christ."

"Bravo! But now tell me why you find this Invitatory psalm put in the third Nocturn; and why is it changed in the form in which we have it there inserted?"

For the first time the youth was stuck. I was sorry for him, but could not tell him that that particular psalm was what might be called a birthmark of Roman ancestry. That does not mean that it is a stain; but it indicates the ancient origin of my Roman lineage, of which I am not a little proud. The Padre had a heart, and seeing the student was embarrassed, he promptly helped him out by saying:

"That is one of the few sections of the Divine Office recited by the Roman clergy, which was kept in its primitive Latin form, of the *Itala*. St. Jerome, in the fifth century, made two successive corrections of the Latin. In the first of these he retained the old text. Subsequently he also made an entirely new translation of the Psalter directly from the Hebrew. It is a testimony to the ancient lineage of the Roman Breviary that it retained the unrevised and earliest text of the Latin Bible in certain parts, among which is this psalm for the feast of the Epiphany. The clergy of those days had been reciting the Psalms from the old Latin version, or *Itala*. The Psalms corrected a second time by St. Jerome, who was not satisfied with his first revision, are known as the Gallican Psalter; these we use today, except for such relics of old custom as the Ninety-fourth Psalm on the feast of the Epiphany."

There was a brief interval, and some of the professors

and students left the hall, though the Examinations were not quite over. After a while all returned and they discussed the *Proprium de Tempore* and the *Proprium Sanctorum*. This was done, not in a devotional fashion, as it is when the Padre takes me up confidentially, but as if I had to be operated on, like a patient under amputation in a dissecting-room.

One of the professors, with stooped shoulders and heavy spectacles, said that my Latinity was poor and ought to be reformed. The idea! As if the prayers that made hundreds of saints out of Popes and Bishops—not to say monks and secular priests, who were surely as smart as he —were not as intelligible before God's throne as if I talked to the Almighty in Ciceronian style!

I admit that I am not perfect, for I am not an angel, but only a Totum, which, like everything earthly, suffers from the defects of this sinful world. My office is precisely to carry messages from sinful men to Heaven, and to bring back messages from the Holy Ghost, for their improvement. Although the offerings of prayer which I have to bear daily to God are not as select and faultless as are the graces which I bring back—since, though everything up in heaven is perfect, human speech is not so—still, there is nothing contraband in my goods. They all have to pass muster at the customhouse office of the Church. They are stamped with the seal of ecclesiastical approbation. Sometimes the officers of the Church at headquarters shut an eye, and let a piece pass through because it is vouched for by a saintly authority or by an old customer. That happens especially in the department of the *Second Nocturn*. The legends of the saints are like their relics. Sometimes they are only secondary articles, that is to say, objects which the saints had merely touched. These parts are of varying perfection, and not all alike in quality or form, but they tend none the less equally to encourage true devotion.

Well, the spectacled professor insisted on showing that in the long past of my ancestral history there had been attempts at what he called "necessary reforms." I maintain that all he showed by his critical questioning was that ancestors of the Totum had been honestly doing their best to offer worthy liturgical worship of God. If they did not completely attain what they aimed at, and if anyone could still point out certain defects in the legends of the saints, it was solely due to the fact that you cannot prevent exaggeration about persons or things which men either admire or hate. Besides, the saints whom the writers of the Second Nocturn picture, were pilgrims on an earthly road, and naturally gathered some dust on their frayed robes. And as these imperfections clung to their persons despite their goodwill and efforts, so they cling to the stories told about them. It is easy enough for a professor in his chair to dogmatize about objective truth and historicity. Let him try to collect historical data on an up-hill road where all kinds of people are throwing dust about them to obscure the truth, and he will soon find out that it is easier to criticize the legends of the Breviary than to ascertain details about the lives of people whose chief virtue was to keep themselves out of sight. These saints wanted to do their good works in the presence of God rather than to be advertised in the newspapers or written about in historical essays by over-smart professors.

At this juncture there was a pause, until the professor of Canon Law, a *Juris Utriusque Doctor,* that is, with J. U. D. after his name, suddenly asked:

"Did you ever hear of the Roman Breviary composed by Cardinal Francis Quiñones?"

The question happened to go to an elderly student who seemed to be considerably in advance of those around him. I believe he was a convert from the Anglican Church, and had actually written about the Roman liturgy when he was still a minister. In truth, they said that it was this very study of the Roman liturgy which led him into the Catholic Church. He seemed quite thoughtful and answered deliberately. It soon became evident that he knew what he was talking about. I liked him, for he spoke as if he had great respect for everything about the Totum. I noticed that he used the word "revision" where the professor had repeatedly said "reform."

VI. Cardinal Quiñones and His Breviary

"The Breviary of Cardinal Quiñones," he answered, "was a revised edition of the older Roman Breviary in use up to the time of the so-called Reformation. It was privately, though rather extensively, circulated for some time during the middle of the sixteenth century. Eventually an order of Pius V (I think in 1568) suppressed it. This Pontiff caused the adoption of the present form of the Roman Office, sanctioned by the Council of Trent."

"Why did Pius V suppress the Quiñones Breviary?" queried the examiner, "I understand that it was quite popular and, owing to its brevity, would have suited our missionary clergy very well."

"Its succinct form did much to recommend it. In truth, some of the Anglican clergy still use a translation of it in English (Cambridge University). But it lacks the admirable traditional features of the older Roman Breviary approved by Nicholas III. It was considered to

CARDINAL QUIÑONES' BREVIARY

present an altogether too drastic change from the previous official liturgy of the Priests' Prayer-book."

"Was there any need of a change such as has already been referred to, or what produced the reform of the Breviary as it was?"

"There had been efforts" was the reply, "at corrections of defects which probably crept into the MS. of the Breviary before the art of printing had come. The later proposals were also, I believe, the result of the tendency of the Renaissance Period under Pope Leo X, to substitute classical forms for what was considered the barbarous Latinity of the current ecclesiastical idiom brought down in the monastic schools from the Middle Ages. Cardinals Bembo, Ferreri, Bessarion and others of the time favored the 'Humanistic movement,' and advocated the cultivation of classical Latinity in the liturgy. As a result, the old hymns were rewritten in the style of Horace, and the Lessons were made to conform to Ciceronian models. The proposed reforms proved, however, distasteful to the men of the older school, like Cardinals Pole, Contarini and Quiñones, and the latter was commissioned to make a new revision. Being a Franciscan, like Pope Nicholas III, he had an eye to the needs of the missionaries, whose days were spent in preaching and whose journeys made canonical prayer difficult. Hence, his aim was to shorten the Offices of the Canonical Prayer. But the Fathers at the Council of Trent argued that missionaries could be dispensed, and that it was essential to clerical perfection that the traditional forms of public prayer should be maintained in the Church."

"And you say, that was done by the Breviary approved at the Council, or by Pius V. Is that the Breviary we have today?"

"Yes, I believe so. With slight alterations. Some of the Lessons, rewritten for the Breviary by Quiñones, were adopted. The sections of Scripture readings for the first Nocturn were taken from the Canon of St. Gregory, and the rhythmic forms of antiphons and responses brought over from the old *Itala* were preserved as best suited to the Gregorian and Ambrosian chants used in the Public Liturgy. There were subsequent revisions or corrections of the text ordered by Clement VIII and Urban VIII in the following century, but they were of minor importance."

"Then, you think there is no need of reforming the Breviary as we have it today!"

I should not say that because the liturgy, like the doctrine of the Church, is progressive in its growth and admits of development. The continuous additions of feasts, to meet new forms of devotion, demand adjustment of the order, and call for elimination of matter that has served its purpose. I imagine it is just like Holy Scripture. There are inspired parts of the Old Testament that have served the purpose of instructing and reforming, for those to whom the lessons were addressed first. These have passed away; and a new generation has need of new prescriptions, though the underlying principles of truth and virtue remain always the same."

"Excellent!" Here the old professor took a pinch of snuff. Now everything was going on smoothly, because the theological student answered in a becoming way which showed his scholarship and also his good sense.

But the old professor who was examining had his notions about reforming me. I suspect he also wanted to show off his learning in ecclesiastical history. One never knows what is going on in the heads of these academic doctors. They remind me of what is written in the first book of the Following of Christ by the venerable monk whom they call Thomas à Kempis, and whom some confound with the great French Chancellor of Paris, whose name was Gerson. He says:

"Scientes libenter volunt videri et sapientes dici," which means that professors like to ask questions in examinations just to let people see, not what the students don't know, but what they themselves, the learned academicians, have studied.

VII. Talks about Reforming the Totum

I was hoping that they would stop, having satisfied themselves that the young theologians knew their matter pretty well. But no. The pinch of snuff seemed to have the effect of making the examiner want to talk more. So he began again:

"One more question: You say liturgy is a progressive science which demands attention to development. Development and progress call for periodical reform. In what, do you think, would the present Roman Breviary need revision or correction, if there were a Council held to father such reform?"

"It would hardly be necessary for the devotional purpose, I believe, which the Roman Breviary actually subserves. But in other respects perfection could be attained probably by a revision, and by a readjustment of the Calendar. The successive introduction of new feasts overcrowds certain portions of the devotional services. Then there is also a need of harmonizing local observances with the universal liturgy. This, in turn, might call for a change of the rubrics in certain parts of the canonical Office."

"Would you think it advisable to make changes in the historic and patristic texts, or even in the Scriptural lessons?"

"Yes, to some extent. Since historical study, as part of the curriculum of study in our theological schools has of late years taken on a critical character, new sources of information are to be found in the freshly-opened record offices of the past. Greater accuracy in regard to matters of fact, such as are connected with the history of the leading heroes of faith whose biographies are read in the Breviary, is possible today, which was not so formerly. This would suggest corrections of data and the elimination of merely legendary accounts which naturally crept into the Breviary composed when critical research in the annals was unknown. The same might be said of the patristic texts. Even the Vulgate Version of the Bible, as originally given us by St. Jerome, is not unlikely to have suffered from inaccuracies of copyists during the many centuries before the art of printing secured for us a permanent text that was safe from interpolations, changes, omissions, or misreadings. So, too, the Gallican Psalter admits of corrections, as is shown in the later new translation by St. Jerome which he made immediately from the Hebrew text."

"Would St. Jerome's final translation of the Psalter from the Hebrew, think you, be an absolutely correct text of the Latin Psalter?"—

Here I came near losing my temper. The querying of the old fogy—though he is, I am sure, a good holy priest, to judge from the deference they show him—seemed to me almost like that of a heretic. The present Psalter has been recited by holy men like St. Martin of Tours down to St. Charles Borromeo, St. Philip de Neri, St. Francis de Sales. It made a saint of the Curé of Ars who, though he is not in my Calendar (he ought to be, and for that I myself favor reform), repeated it daily on his knees, as did many a holy cleric during the last thousand years. If it was good enough for them, it ought to be so for these modernists who talk of nothing but progress, by which they mean merely acceptance of new fangled notions, which is not at all the same thing! But the Totum's business is to give the priest a piece of its mind only in the regular canonical order, that is in the Homilies.

And these ill-tempered thoughts of mine about the cranky professor could not be printed; accordingly I held them down. "In patientia vestra!" says St. Paul.

The Padre kept quiet and held me under his thumb; otherwise I might have burst with indignation, or fallen off the table in a fit despite any good resolutions. However, it was near dinner time, and I knew that the hunger or thirst for displaying wisdom about the insides of the Totum was not likely to make them forget the Angelus bell, with the meal immediately following. But the convert student did not seem to be in the least excited, so that I felt a bit ashamed, though nobody could have seen it, even while they were dissecting my insides. He answered composedly:

"St. Jerome's translation from the Hebrew Psalter might call for comparison with the Septuagint Greek text, which is probably older than the Hebrew copy which he had before him, since it the Septuagint version was made at least two centuries before Christ, and had the approval of the Jews at Alexandria, if not also that of the Jerusalem Sanhedrin. Besides, the Hebrew script had only the consonant letters written out, allowing the vowel pronunciation to be supplied for the reader by local tradition. It is not improbable that the Latin translation of the Psalter which St. Jerome made, showed the influence of rabbinical prejudices which the saint had imbibed. Meanwhile the Greek version was used by most of the

Christians in their religious services and particularly in arguments to prove to Jewish proselytes the Messianic fulfilment. St. Jerome, whilst he sympathized naturally with the Christian interpretation, was nevertheless bent upon getting what he thought to be the genuine Hebrew text (the *Hebraica veritas*), and as he learned his Hebrew from Jewish masters, he trusted their reading probably more than that of the Septuagint. The latter has been used in the various revisions of the Psalter such as we have it in the Breviary at present."

"*Bene dixisti—recte loquasti,*" said the professor. I think it was bad Latin; but I am not quite sure of it. I don't use such expressions in my talk with the Lord, or for the instruction and edification of clerics. But the old modernist examiner had the floor, and though I was getting warmed up under the hold which the Padre had of me, I kept my peace and waited for my master to express his views. What surprised me was that he seemed to be delighted with the whole proceeding, and shook hands with the convert, who appeared to have been selected for promotion by reason of his superior knowledge as well as ripe judgment.

Then they all went out talking and laughing, as if the examinations had merely been fun.

Fifth Part

I. THE SEVEN HOURS OF THE DIVINE OFFICE

AT THE next lecture the Padre told the students that the Totum bore the impress of the Divine Spirit. Besides the "Imprimatur" of the Popes and Cardinals on its front page, it had the hallmark of Heaven, which meant the signed approbation of God the Father, Son and Holy Ghost.

That mark appears in the number *seven*. The Breviary is the seven-days' work of the Holy Trinity. Seven was a sacred number among the chosen people of God in the Old Law. It is the symbol of Divine Perfection, expressed or combined with earthly completeness or perfection in the material order.

"You see," he said, "the number three, being the symbol of the Holy Trinity, means perfection in God. *Omne Trinum perfectum* was of old applied as equivalent to saying that a thing which expressed the number three had the approval of God. Hence the law courts of the Romans (as Neratius Priscus informs us in his *Digesta* accepted it as an axiom, meaning that the judgment or evidence of three witnesses, or the agreement of three judges, established the right of a sentence. They expressed it by the saying, *'Tres faciunt collegium,'* and the dictum became a byword in the schools and at the universities as equivalent to a decision, whenever the absence of hearers at a professor's lecture caused a doubt whether or not he was obliged to lecture. If there were at least three students present he was obliged by the academic rules to give the lecture; otherwise he was free.

The same was applied to the recitation in choir of the canonical Offices."

Just as the number three stands for Trinity and symbolizes Divine Perfection, so four suggests the material order, symbolized by the square or four sides of an equilateral plane figure with its four equal angles. It always stands right; its base on the ground; which means that it is the proper material foundation expressing fundamental order.

Now, the three and the four combined make a sacramental completeness or perfection in which the Divine joins with the earthly or the spiritual with the material. Just as this union of the three and four produces the sacramental order of a heavenly grace conferred by an outward sign on matter and form, so the spiritual forces of prayer combine in the Canonical Prayer (which is the Totum—me) with the voice and tongue of man, bringing down the grace of God.

Thus, he showed them how in the Breviary there was a power of inspired thought, and how Holy Mother Church both expresses that power, and answers to it in the Latin tongue, the language of Rome.

That was not all. He next pointed out how the Church kept in mind the injunction of Our Lord to pray always. By making prayer sevenfold she makes it continuous; for the seven hours of the Divine Office are but the impulses that set the current of heavenly aspirations and breathings of grateful and eucharistic chant in motion, creating a continuous action. "Seven times each day I have uttered praise to Thee, O Lord," says the psalmist (Ps. 118:164). Since the psalm is both a prophecy and the recitation of a perpetual law, it means that praise of God in the mouth of His servants is to be continuous through all time. The seven days of the week

THE SEVEN HOURS OF THE OFFICE 117

symbolizing the creative action of God, with the Sabbath of rest, were to be wholly devoted to a continuous service expressed in the command given to the Levites of old: "Seven days thou shalt offer holocaust to the Lord" (Lev. 23:7 and 35).

In conformity with this expression of the Divine Will, the Church has ingeniously adapted the round of her annual cycle in such a way as to reflect seven periods in the life of Christ on earth:

1. Preparation (Advent).
2. Childhood and youth (Christmas and Epiphany cycle).
3. Public Life (covering the period between Pentecost and Advent, when the Church rehearses the actions and doctrines of Christ on successive Sundays).
4. Passiontide (with its preparation of Lent).
5. Death, and the Institution of the Holy Sacrifice in which that Oblation is repeated.
6. Resurrection, with the Paschal cycle until
7. Pentecost and the establishment of the Church.

Such is the circle of devotional action in the Church, through which she is guided by the Totum. Think of it! Every day I lead the priest to the altar steps with Matin service and Lauds, with morning prayer of Prime and Terce. I take with me the Saint of the day, or several of them, or a chorus of Angels helps me to direct the chant of the priests everywhere from morn to nightfall, in honor of the Divine Mysteries and Mercy. And the harmony of the chant, of the Psalter, the variety of the adornment, and the beauty of the Church's raiment, which is the manifold virtue of her canonized Children, is rehearsed day by day, through all the months and seasons of the ecclesiastical year.

When God created the world of light, He began to draw it out of darkness. "All was void and empty, and darkness was upon the face of the deep." At the end of the first day of light came the evening. Hence, when He gave His law to Moses He said, "From evening until evening you shall celebrate your sabbaths" (Lev. 23:32).

Accordingly, the daily canonical service of divine worship in the Christian Church begins with evening—that is, with Vespers—and in a way sets the example of regularity in the priestly life.

I wonder if priests are more sleepy at the present time than they used to be. The Americans are lively enough, and pretty hard workers, if I may judge from the Padre and the way he makes the students hustle. He does not always go to bed at nine, which is the regulation hour in the Seminary for putting out the lights. But, then, he anticipates Matins and Lauds. He knows that he should have to get up to recite them during the night, if he were a monk. Hence he does the Nocturns betimes, so as not to be caught napping as the monks do sometimes in their stalls. In Belgium, where I come from, there are religious priests, and also cloistered nuns, who are very particular about the recital of the Divine Office. They chant:

Vespers and *Compline* between 6 and 9 o'clock in the evening;
Matins, which they divide into the
First Nocturn, between 9 and 12 o'clock at night;
Second Nocturn, between 12 and 2 A.M., when the cock crows (gallicinium);
Third Nocturn, between 3 and 6 o'clock in the morning. Hence it is called "hora matutina." Then they immediately chant :

Lauds. This is the morning praise. The old Benedictine rule says, "incipiente luce decantatur hymnus quidam gaudii ad celebrandas Dei Laudes."
Next come:
Prime,
Terce,
Sext,
None.

These last offices are short because the monks and priests have to work during the day. The prayer is thus done in great part at night. This is following Our Lord's example, of whom it is said repeatedly "erat pernoctans in oratione"; whereas during the day, Christ preached to the people and healed the sick.

The most interesting part of a Totum, said the Padre, is this, that it does not simply urge clerics to pray, but that it tells them stories; every day a new one, either from the Bible history or from profane annals and martyrologies. These cover the period from the persecutions by the Roman Emperors and all through the struggles toward Christianity during the Middle Ages. The lessons are often quite dramatic and include heroes and heroines from all classes of people and from every country. Moreover, the language is, for the most part, of the classical type, both in prose and poetry; though some of the stories are told in the "lingua vulgaris or plebeja" of the time and place in which the incidents related occurred.

So there you are. The people who think I am just a prayerbook written in barbarous ecclesiastical Latin are all wrong, for the Padre is a good judge. Why, I saw for myself one day, when he dumped me unceremoniously down on his writing-desk, how he wrote out lines of poetry on a blank sheet, which he afterward corrected and put in a separate portfolio with the inscription, "Personal Papers," and having his initials on the cover. I believe that I often suggest to him the composition of Latin verses, for he sometimes interrupts conversation with me, and all at once begins to write. After a while he takes me up again. Of course he is never rude, so as to do this in the middle of a psalm or lesson; but as soon as there is a reasonable break in the Office, he is apt to go off into reveries which make him write poetry. Sometimes he consults another book in between, and I should think it a case of alienation of affections that might make one jealous, if it were not that he evidently comes back, and lets me feel that he owes his inspirations to me. I can trust him; for I know he loves the Church, and therefore the Breviary—that is, the Totum—better than his poetry or anything on earth.

II. The Gallican and the Roman Psalter

These American students are fine lads, intelligent, and perfectly frank in the way they ask questions. The Professor evidently likes them much better than he likes the Belgians, though I heard him say that the latter are better trained in the rudiments, more composed, and not as noisy.

When the Padre had explained that the Scripture stories always come first in Matins, beginning with Genesis on Septuagesima Sunday, and that the entire course of the Breviary is in reality a series of instructive and at the same time "Entertaining Varieties," one of the theologians in the front row laughed right out. The Padre was not a bit displeased, but smiled and said:

"Yes, a regular entertainment, to which you get a

special invitation each day. You see it begins with *Venite, exultemus,* which means, 'Come to the frolic,' and sing with joy: 'Jubilemus Domino.'

"Then follows immediately a hymn in honor of the president, or the flag, or the army—like *Iste Confessor,* or *Rex sempiterne,* or *Vexilla Regis,* when used as a processional hymn—or *Deus tuorum militum,* and so on; all of which emphasizes, in the first place, as it ought, the genuine patriotism of the Catholic priest.

"Next comes a trio of psalms, and then the story from the inspired classics. That completes the First Nocturn, or the first act of the entertainment."

The clerics were here reminded that the Psalms are Gallican, as the Gallicans were the first to monopolize the Latin revision by St. Jerome. After that, they foisted them on the Romans and the rest of the world. The French have always been rather tenacious of their local traditions. At one time they wanted to make the whole Church Gallican; that is, they set up a Peter's Chair for themselves. Before that, they had actually transported the Popes to Avignon; and if it had not been for that clever and courageous nun, St. Catherine of Siena, maybe we should all be getting our orders still from France.

A junior theologian in one of the front seats wanted to ask a question, and when the Professor assented, he blustered out:

"Mine, Sir, is a *Roman* Breviary, printed in Rome; and the Psalms are exactly like those in Pat's Breviary, which was printed at Tours in France."—As he said this he pointed to his neighbor, who had a Pars Verna in his hand. It was evident that these two clerics had been reciting the Office together from their different books. This drew a smile from the Professor.

"The Psalter which you have in the Roman Breviary,"

explained the Padre, "is called the Gallican Psalter, as I explained before, simply because it was adopted in France before it was popularized and prescribed in Rome. The Roman clergy were in the habit of using an older Latin psalter before the bishops of the French dioceses found that there was a more correct version of the psalms. These were revised twice by St. Jerome. At Rome the priests had been reciting the canonical psalms, from the first revision, which was made of an old translation called the *Itala*. The *Itala* was originally made for the clergy in Africa, where Latin was more common in the Church service than Greek, before the time of St. Augustine. It was not very good Latin. Pope St. Damasus, who was a classical scholar, desired to have the Offices recited correctly in the principal church of Rome. Since he did not approve of the African translation, or *Itala*, he commissioned St. Jerome, who was his Latin secretary and who knew Greek and Latin well, to revise the old *Itala*. When that was completed, the Roman clergy were instructed to commit it to memory, for use in the canonical services. This was done immediately, and the clergy of St. Peter's in Rome to this day retain that particular revision of the psalter in the recitation of the Breviary. After St. Damasus had died, St. Jerome went to pursue Biblical studies in Palestine. He had got a glimpse at Cesarea of Origen's famous Hexapla. Comparing the Greek text with his first revision, he realized that he had overlooked certain corrections, in his earlier work. Then he set to work and made a second revision, which he sent to Rome. This second Latin version was not at once adopted by the Roman clergy, partly because it involved a change which could not be made without authoritative enactment from the Pope, and partly because the older clergy were loath to adopt a new version which required fresh memory effort and was in no wise essential to the reverent worship to which they were addicted. Our Roman Missal and even the Breviary, as well as the Milanese Liturgy, still retain traces of the old version, and illustrate the conservative spirit in the Church, which preserves at least in part, the text of St. Jerome's first effort at revising the Latin *Itala*.

"But when the bishops of Gaul and Spain, and later of Germany, came to Rome to make their visits *ad limina*, and to seek to model their practices after those of the Mother Church, they were instructed to avail themselves of the second and more correct version rather than follow the earlier readings as revised by St. Jerome. Thus it happened that the second revision was adopted in the churches of Gaul, and, although subsequently used also by the Roman clergy, it became known under the name of Gallican Psalter.

"Years after this, when St. Jerome had perfectly mastered the Hebrew tongue, he was not content with either of his earlier revisions and made an entirely new translation. This has never been popularized, and our Vulgate still contains the second revision."

III. The Second Nocturn

Today I learnt a lesson of humility. The Padre spent the entire hour in criticizing me and pointing out my imperfections. I had felt rather flattered when in his previous lecture he had said that I was a work of art, and that whilst not every part of me was actually inspired, like the Psalms and Scripture lessons, still the hymns, homilies and prayers were fine models of classical composition. About the stories of the saints which come in the Second Nocturn, when even pious monks and clerics are usually sleepy and begin to nod, he had said that they were not all literally and historically true in details. But, then, that was not anything wrong. These stories are told for edification, not to be criticized as historical facts. The essential value of the lessons is not to be sought in the names, dates and chronological order of events, but in the moral, together with the ideals, set forth in the examples. Truth may be taught by legend, no less than by exact science or by history. The Parables used by Our Lord, and indeed much of the Scriptural history, are to be taken figuratively, not literally.

Well, with this I thought, of course, that nothing could be said against me, either on the score of devotion, art, or history. All of a sudden the Padre stated that, although the Breviary had gone through many corrections in its long life, still it needed more. Then he went into some details about which the less said, I thought, the better. The Padre mixed up Councils and Popes and all sorts of clerics, and even some kings, in what seemed to me disreputable squabbles about the Breviary. He also quoted what different learned and unlearned people thought it ought to be.

The Professor had announced that he would not go into the history of the subject; but now he switched off anyhow. I could see, of course, what he meant. He really wanted to show off the excellencies of the Totum. I have naturally a desire for perfection; for I am not just a prayer-machine. I am an intelligent moral personality, like the Church herself, endowed with faculties of mind and heart; and I have a body too, which means that I can grow. If Our Lord, the God-Man, could be said to grow in grace as well as in age, there is no discredit in allowing that a Totum may grow in perfection. That means, naturally, that there must be a state of temporary imperfection whence the desire of greater perfection arises. It is the human element in me, the body, so to speak, that needs occasional setting right, cleaning up, and examination for proper exercise, or tests of practical application.

The fact is, I confess it, that the Pope, some time ago, said that I needed reform. That settles it. What Pope Pius IX, who was devoted to me, and always treated me or my family with great respect, did in 1856 was to appoint a Commission to examine whether the reform of the Breviary were opportune or not. That supposed the need of a reform. But when it came to what the revision was to correct, or change, it developed that the views of supposed experts greatly differed. It was a question, largely, of private judgment, such as influenced the opinions of the so-called reformers of the sixteenth century in regard to the Bible. The French bishops, as usual, wanted everything to be done in the French fashion. They demanded expurgation of the apocryphal matter in the Lessons, rewriting of the hymns in a purely classical and polished style of the Augustan age, greater variation in the distribution of the psalms. They complained also that there were too many Roman saints in the Calendar (which meant too few French), and they said that the Office was altogether too long for busy missionaries like themselves, especially on Sundays. The Canadians joined this proposal, and asked for a shortening of the Office on all the eves of great festivals, when priests would be engaged in the ministry of souls more than on other days.

The German and Italian Bishops called, in the main, for exactness in historical and exegetical matter. One reform asked for by the General of the Minims, Father

Raffaelo Ricea, was to reduce the Office to a uniform set of readings and prayers, to be said by every cleric, secular or religious, throughout the world. The General had more piety and charity than wisdom. I, for one, would protest against being despoiled of the gift of beauty, which consists of variety in unity, by having my mind and heart paralyzed by the mechanical dronings of the same daily exercise, which would soon become a mere feat of memory and vocal repetitions.

All these schemes were to be discussed at a General Vatican Council which was never concluded. Well, it may be done yet. The Fathers who afterward met at Rome, had not time; so they put it off. But some later Pope, perhaps the present one, will surely take it up. It won't matter to me, for I am on the shelf for my Requiem æternam now, and Totums are almost forgotten with the making of new books.

IV. THE GREGORIAN METHOD TO BE UPSET

Speaking of reforms and revisions, the Padre gave his own notions. Considering that he is an American, and they seem to be always ahead, I have an idea that his views for my improvements are not so bad, and will probably be shared by other Churchmen who have the influence to introduce them.

First of all, the Professor spoke of the Calendar. That too needs, it appears, reform. He had discussed the topic before, with reference to the form adopted by Gregory XIII and the peculiarities of the Dominical and Golden Letters and the Epacts. But this time he spoke of the necessity of a uniform calendar that would simplify the keeping of counts, and our relations to the secular world.

THE GREGORIAN METHOD 127

It would be an advantage to have Easter all ways occur on a fixed day, and to have all the days of the year recur with their dates on the same day of the week. That requires an even number of weeks making up the year. If we have seven days to the week and three hundred and sixty-five days to the year we get fifty-two weeks with a surplus of one day or a little more at the end of the solar year. That surplus day would have to be added on to one of the regular fifty-two weeks, and thus give us a week of eight days at least once a year. The objection to this is, that such a week of eight days would be contrary to the Sabbath ordinance, which rests upon Divine precept. Someone has, however, suggested that the intercalary day could be ignored until it summed up to seven, and then a full week added to the cycle would cause no interference with the Sabbath ordinance. The Professor favored this reform, as it simplifies the mutual relations of religious and civil life, and establishes a time measure that could be foreseen without intricate scientific calculation.

One of the students here proposed the question: "But is not the Easter date fixed by the Scriptures as dependent upon the full moon and the vernal equinox? And if so, how could Easter Sunday be placed in the fifty-two weeks' scheme so as to recur on the same date each year?"

To this the Padre replied that the Easter, or Pasch, of the Jews which determines our present ecclesiastical observance of Easter Sunday, is not based upon a directly Divine ordinance, but had its origin in a conventional Jewish arrangement by which the Hebrews who came to celebrate the Paschal feast at Jerusalem would be allowed to travel at night, with the light of the moon aiding them in their journey. It was difficult, on account of the heat and the dust of the roads in Palestine at this season, to travel by day. The nocturnal dew and the full moonlight at night facilitated the movements of the caravans that came from long distances. Hence, Easter Sunday might be fixed on a Sunday suitable to any scheme without violating a Biblical law. It was merely a question of doing away with precedent and long tradition.

"Well, some day the change will probably be made. But that is a while off, and won't interfere with my service and present superiority."

V. "Confitemini Domino"

At last the Examinations are over. Deo gratias! It was harder on the Totum than it could possibly have been on the candidates for Holy Orders. The professors treated me as if I were a catalogue at an auction sale of old books. They were looking for the answers to their propositions, just as an auctioneer looks for an indication of the highest figure among the bidders. It certainly tested my equanimity, though they could not, of course, lower my sense of the dignity of a Roman Breviary. It is a title which the Popes have bestowed on Totums, just as they crowned emperors and kings since the days of Constantine, I believe.

But the next day the Padre brought the young clerics back to their senses. He told them that the Examinations, while they were tests of intelligence and application to the required theological studies, in preparation for the priestly office, were by no means the end and purpose of their knowledge regarding the Divine Office.

They had mastered something of the mechanism of the heavenly act. They had rehearsed the parts of the speakers in the great drama to be enacted in the court of the King of kings, in presence of the angels and saints, and for the benefit of the faithful and the children of God throughout the world. The chief purpose of the Canonical Office was still to be established; that was, to put the proper spirit into the recitation of the Breviary.

This spirit was not alone one of reverence and piety or devotion. It was a certain enthusiasm which comes with the realization of the part which the priest or cleric, in reciting the daily Office, plays as an ambassador of Christ. When the cleric takes up his Totum for the recitation of the Canonical Hours each day, he steps out before an audience which expects to admire, to be moved, to applaud with cordial enthusiasm. Accordingly his acting, like his words, must reflect the part he plays in the *Divina Commedia*. The effect on those to whom and for whom he acts and prays must be a contagion of the aspirations and passion expressed in what he utters, in the appeal he makes through his recitatives.

The animation of the act appears first of all in the *Psalms*. They are, for the most part, appeals, in which a number of *dramatis persona*, whom he cites, take part. At times the psalms represent monologues. There are also choruses, in which the chief actor gives the intonations and calls for the repetitions. Take, for example, the psalm recited on the morning of the regular Sunday Office, which begins:

Confitemini Domino quoniam bonus, quoniam in sæculum misericordia ejus.[6]

The priest stands before the faithful as did the chief of the Levites in the sanctuary among the sons of Core, in the days of Israel's Tabernacle. After intoning the

---

[6] Ps. 117, Vulgate.

above chant, inviting all to the praise of the Lord God because He is kind, and because His mercy endureth forever, the priestly psalmist calls on the congregation:

Dicat nunc Israel quoniam bonus; quoniam in sæculum misericordia ejus.

Then he turns to the house of Aaron:

Dicat nunc domus Aaron: quoniam in sæculum misericordia ejus.

Finally he addresses all who fear God; those, namely, who are not of the fold of Israel, nor of the house of Aaron, but who hearken to the voice of conscience—men of good will, to whom the message of peace is announced with the coming of Christ.

Dicant nunc qui timent Dominum: quoniam in sæculum misericordia ejus.

In the verses that follow, the priest utters his own heart's desires for the salvation of the people.

Similarly, the entire range of psalms may be analyzed, to find the dramatic element which makes of them an action, instead of a mere verbal recitation.

Such is indeed the fundamental notion of the whole psalm series. They are actions not simply words. To realize this, one must study them. And there the cleric finds the proper material for his meditation, as a preparation for the Holy Sacrifice of the Altar, with its introduction of the Divine Office for each day.

The Hebrew word *Mizmor,* which is translated *Psalmos* by the Greek interpreters, has the meaning of a song accompanied by musical instruments (stringed). But the contents of the Psalter, as we have it in the Breviary, cover an even wider range. They present, as Flavius Josephus explains, "hymns in honor of God, and precepts

"CONFITEMINI DOMINO" 131

of right living" (Ap. I, 8). We have something analogous in the medieval concept of the so-called "Morality Plays," or, in a kindred sense, of the poems of Dante, the Vita Nuova, and the plays of Shakespeare. A section of the Hebrew Psalter has the subscription *Thephiloth*, in which *prayer* is the chief note, including appeal to mercy, Eucharistic praise, and thanksgiving. St. Jerome and Eusebius transliterate the same title into *Sephar Tallim*, which, broadly, means Song of Praise.

The separate title of *Mizmor* indicates a musical recitative, or, also, a symphony with accompaniment of harp and zithern. The title is given distinctly to fifty-seven of the psalms, as they are grouped in our Psalter today. These are definitely religious or devotional. Other parts are grouped under the title *Shir,* which ordinarily applies to secular poetry. The theocratic idea, which made all of Israel's concerns part of the religious cult, is indicated by the combination of titles *shir mizmor* attached to a number of the Psalm texts in Hebrew.

The Psalms were differently grouped, from time to time, in the history of the Jewish people, to suit the liturgical purpose of the temple service and of the various synagogues later, in the dispersion of the exiled tribes. Great events of triumph, of national mourning, of renewed Messianic hopes, were commemorated by a new adaptation of the Psalm tones.

In the Totum they are arranged, without textual changes, to suit the festive cycle of the ecclesiastical year.

All this was explained by the Padre, who held me in his left hand, near his heart, the whole time while he spoke to the students. He told them that it was impossible, during the short period that remained before the Retreat, to enter into an exegesis of the psalms separately. That was to be done by themselves. There were books, commentaries in Latin and in the vernacular tongues, which would help them, and he hoped that every one of the *ordinandi* would keep on his desk a copy of some such commentary and read, or study, the psalms as they occurred in the daily Office of the Breviary. It would serve not only to make their recital of the Canonical Hours *digne, attente ac devote,* but also to broaden their view of life; for the Psalter contains the history of the soul, and from it issues the secret of light by which the ministry of God's priests becomes fruitful and practical, while it indicates the model upon which the children of God are to reform their lives, and to sanctify them. Hence the Psalter ends in the hundred, and fiftieth song with the words

> Let everything that hath the breath of life in it
> Ring the praise of God!

Someone among the *ordinandi* asked the Professor about the hundred and fifty-first psalm.

"That is an addition which does not belong to the original Hebrew liturgical collection, although it is found in the Septuagint and some Latin versions. Probably it pertains to the composition of Syrian or Aramaic writings which, like the Hebrew and Greek *Apocrypha,* were intended to fill in the supposed historical gaps in the Canon of Esdras. The psalm is, as I may have mentioned before, composed in Greek, and has a prefatory note stating that it was written by David after he had slain Goliath in single combat, although it is outside the number (hundred and fifty, which was believed to be sacred and symbolical)."

When the Padre returned the following day to continue his instruction to the young levites, on the

Totum, he brought the Latin text of the so-called hundred and fifty-first psalm with him, and a translation in English. I was glad he did not read it in Latin, for anybody could tell that it does not belong to my collection of the Gallican Psalter. The style would itself show that it is not genuine Hebrew poetry. But he gave them the English version, and they were pleased to copy it. I had it for a while between my leaves in the Padre's own handwriting; and although it does not belong to me, I give it here as a matter of literary curiosity:

> The youngest in my father's house
> I lived among my brethren,
> Guarding afield our flocks of sheep.
> The while they grazed I made the harp
> And fashioned with my hands the lyre—
> To sing the praises of the Lord,
> For none is like Him, Who our prayers hears.
> He sent His angel to withdraw
> Me from the shepherding at home;
> Caused me to be anointed
> With chrysm of the royal state.
> Although my brethren were more strong
> And tall than I, the Lord left them.
> And bade me meet the Philistine
> Who cursed me by his idols vain.
> Then did I draw his sword from him
> And cut his head from off his neck,
> Whereon the shame of our defeat
> Was taken from Israel's sons.

VI. "Beatus Vir"

"I shall give you a brief analysis of the first psalm," said the Professor, "which forms an Introduction to the entire canonical collection of the fifty liturgical psalms, and it opens the musical chant of the Divine Office."

At last we were back to the very heart of the Totum. I had had some fears that he would say nothing about my real insides—I mean my soul; for of course, that is what counts. Thus far, the whole talk had been about my structure, the physical organism. Very little had been said about my disposition, which is really lovely, although there are clerics, I think, who don't appreciate me because they don't fully know me. They have a notion that I am a sort of imposition, a companion they cannot get rid of easily, who follows them like a private detective. Well, I cannot help being misunderstood. But the Padre is giving me a lift, and tries to put me in the proper light before these young men. God bless him!

The first thing he wished to do, he said, was to give them an Introduction to me. That was his politeness. He knew it would be a mistake to introduce me to them, though that is what these young clerics did really expect. Like all other people who are called to important positions, they are a bit conceited and expect everybody to bow to them. Well, that may come later. Just now he called each of them by name *Beatus vir*.

"That is your prerogative," he said. "Privileged and blessed is he who is called to associate with the Totum, to be admitted to the Divine Presence, to converse with God, and plead for the world as His ambassador!

"The election and function of the *Beatus vir* requires certain qualifications. In the first place, he must be free from a disposition to get into bad company, or to seek the patronage of wrongdoers; and, most of all, he has to keep from getting into their habits so as to teach evil to others by his example.

"The next requisite is that he have a good disposition; that he know and observe the urbanities and rules of propriety required in the King's household; and, finally, that he be ready for the royal service at any hour, night or day."

To give them a sort of picture of what is expected of them as embodiments of the *Beatus vir* he drew an outline on the blackboard in the classroom, which marked the points of negative and positive qualification in each. It looked this way when written out:

> *Beatus vir* qui
> 1. *Non abiit* in consilio impiorum; et
> 2. *Non stetit* in via peccatorum; et
> 3. *Non sedit* in cathedra pestilentiæ
> sed
> 1. *Voluntas* ejus in lege Domini; et
> 2. *Meditabitur* in lege ejus;
> 3. *Die ac nocte.*

"First of all," he said, "you notice the triple negative. The man whom the Lord calls *blessed* (beatus), the man who is, as it were canonized by the Holy Ghost—that is to say, the levite, the cleric called to the sacred office of the priesthood, in which all blessedness concentrates, and who expects to possess and to dispense the choice treasures of God's grace and wealth, must avoid three things, be free from three habits of worldliness.

"These imply: motion, standing still, and settling down in certain conditions of life against which God fights. They compose that world of men for which Christ has no use among His apostles, as when He said to them: 'I pray for you, I pray not for the world.'

"Now, the secular, who is excluded from participation in Christ's prayer and company, is the man (qui abiit in consolio impiorum) who runs about consulting with worldlings, is busy about concerns that are purely temporal and has a habit of making trouble for his superiors. He belongs to that class of restless clerics who are rarely at home, and yet whose wanderings abroad are not after the lost or straying sheep of the flock, but after secular diversions and friendships; for such is the meaning of *impiorum.*

"The psalmist wishes to warn the reader not merely against wasting time and talents in idle gossipings and goings abroad, but against settling down to a low standard of life, making sin a habit from which it is difficult to recover before the hour of death. Such is the man who

Stetit in via peccatorum

Note the change from *abiit* to *stetit,* and also that of *consilio impiorum* to *via peccatorum.* If the first step toward adopting a wrong course of life, which precludes the blessed realization of the priestly graces, is that of going abroad and listening to the advice of those who lack piety, the next step means the becoming familiar with and fixed in habits of sin.

"The last stage of the downward course consists in becoming a teacher as well as a doer of wrong. This is expressed by the figure of him who

Sedit in cathedra pestilentiæ

The word *pestilentiæ* here has the sense of the

scorner's attitude, the cynic who ridicules virtue, inculcates wrong principles and scandalizes the weak while corrupting the young."

After this pen-picture of what the cleric who cultivates the acquaintance of the Totum must *not* be, the Professor drew another outline on the blackboard, showing what are the positive qualities that procure a lasting friendship through familiar intercourse with the Breviary.

"The three qualities that signalize the devout ecclesiastic in Holy Orders are:

Good-will, that is, a disposition to observe the law of God. This is what the words:

> 1. *voluntas ejus in lege Domini,* imply.

The habitual inclinations of the true priest are in the direction of order, right and justice—the higher spiritual aspirations which make for the observance of God's laws. This disposition, or inclination to find, and do, the nobler things—to avoid sin, grow in virtue, and increase the kingdom of God and His glory—has, however, to be fostered and sustained. This is done by reflection. Hence, blessedness is promised him who

> 2. *meditabitur in lege Domini*

Meditation here is more than simple reflection. The Hebrew word suggests action and speech together with thought. It has much the force of the word *psallere,* akin to *mizmor,* and is applied to a person who talks things over with himself in a singing fashion, as if to indicate a joyous motive, a resolution taken with alacrity, to do God's holy will and promote His glory among those who can and will hear Him. When such action is made the constant and supreme effort of the will, so that it occupies the mind and heart

3. *die ac nocte,*

and not merely spasmodically, then it secures the blessedness promised to the faithful cleric, the true man whom the psalmist has in mind."

The students were all very attentive. They were to enter the Retreat for the spiritual exercises preparatory to the Ordination in a few days, and they realized the importance of what the Padre said.

He went on after that to show them how the psalmist was not satisfied with merely prescribing what was to be avoided and what was to be done, if they wanted to be on friendly terms with the Totum. The inspired writer proceeded immediately to illustrate his precepts, much as Our Lord Himself was in the habit of doing when He spoke to the people in parables and figures.

"The friends of the Breviary who wish to earn the approbation and gain the merit of reciting the Divine Office properly, are like a tree planted by the riverside and giving promise of fruit at the time of ripening and harvest. The most favored image of spiritual blessedness and perfection among the Hebrews was that of a tree. Every variety of attributes, such as gracefulness, beauty, productiveness, immortality, is symbolized by the cedars of Lebanon, the palms of Cades, the cypress of Sion. Not only are these applied to the Wisdom which exhibits the Divine Spirit in His Creation, but by the Christian interpreters, to Our Blessed Lady, and to the Church of Christ.

"In this case they embody the beauty, grace and perfection of the life of the priest who draws waters from the Savior's fountains and brings forth worthy fruit in his ministry, such as the apostolic mission demands.

Ut eatis et fructum afferatis

Et fructus vester maneat.

In such fashion does the psalmist sketch the *Beatus vir* when he says:

> *Erit tamquam lignum plantatum*
> *Secus decursus aquarum, quod*
> *Fructum dabit in tempore suo.*

"Not merely is his work to be presently successful, but it is to be lasting for generations, down the eternal years, multiplying long after the tree itself has grown old and decayed! For no leaf shall be lost, and prosperity shall crown the future growth, since the seed springs perennial, unfolding new gifts with each returning spring season. To such there is no failure.

> *Folium ejus non defluet; et*
> *Omnia quacumque faciet, prosperabuntur.*

"By way of contrast the divine poet pictures the default and ultimate worthlessness, weighed in the balance of God's justice, of the sinner, or rather of the priest lacking the piety which is the demand of his state and profession. There is a dramatic insistence in the expression

> *Non sic impii, non sic—*

The triviality of the man without devotion is compared to the chaff which like dust is driven before the wind. The comparison is taken from the harvest scene, as if to point out the absence of all fruit in the granary of the husbandman, or the sower of seed in the field of the Lord. The hirelings are like the scattered straw— worthless, *Tamquam pulvis,* and they are driven before the wind, just as they had been moved by every gust of allurement in their pastoral career:

140 AUTOBIOGRAPHY OF AN OLD BREVIARY

quem projicit ventus a facie terra.

Their end is hopeless, for the Lord will not forget. They shall not rise on judgment day, with the counsel of the just, because God will not know them as Blessed."

There was clapping of hands when he was done, which was unusual. But they were no longer mere students. had shown them that they were on the eve of being elected friends of Christ:

Non vos vocarem servos, sed amicos,

—and that meant, of course, that I was to be the intermediary through whose friendship they would be perpetually united with their Divine Master.

He had not much time left to explain further about the history of the psalm. But he said that it had been composed as a Foreword to the liturgical chanting in the Tabernacle and temple, and that it formed a sort of Key to the entire psalter contained in the Totum.

There were two more days, when he hoped to complete his talk about the Divine Office. But that did not mean rest for the Totum.

VII. The Bishop Examines

The Bishop came out to the Seminary today. He wanted to see the candidates for Ordination and have a talk with each of them separately. The Bishop is very particular, as I noticed when he sat down in the Padre's library, and asked him questions about the young men before he spoke to them. He had a book from which he read notes about things he had apparently heard from the pastors regarding the character, habits, family connections and personal gifts or dispositions of some of

THE BISHOP EXAMINES

the aspirants for priestly orders.

I was lying on the prie-dieu in my customary attitude of close attention, and heard everything that passed between His Lordship, the Padre, and later before the students. The two superiors would discuss each candidate before he was called into the room to be quizzed by the Bishop, but the rector retired into an adjoining room while the former examined the young men alone. One point which the Bishop emphasized in each case was the relation of pastor and curate.

"I understand that you have read and studied the Statutes of the Diocese. What would you do if there arose in your mind a doubt regarding the interpretation of certain diocesan statutes, in which you found that your pastor differed from the view you had regarding the extent of its obligation or its application under certain circumstances?"

"I should follow the view which I was taught in the Seminary, or which I found in approved authors to be the right one."

"You might modify that viewpoint, Sir, and obey your pastor. He is likely to know the law, and its application by experience, better than you."

"But might he not be wrong, my Lord?"

"Yes, he might be; but the presumption is that he is right. If you should have serious doubt about it, so as to make it a question of conscience or sin on your part to obey, then put the matter before your Bishop and abide by his decision, which relieves you from further responsibility."

In another case, where the student showed a tendency to insist on canonical rights in connection with the possession of privileged faculties, the Bishop, asked:

"Curates have certain rights, have they not?"

"Oh, yes, my Lord."

"For instance, the taking of a vacation each year.—Suppose your pastor, for reasons that affect the administration of the parish—such as his own temporary inability to do pastoral duty without the aid of an assistant, or to supply a needed service for the congregation—were to refuse you leave to absent yourself from the parish for the purpose of a vacation. Would you insist on taking your vacation?"

"No, unless I saw that the pastor could do without me."

"And if the pastor maintained that he could not do without you?"

"In that case I might get a substitute during my absence."

"And if the pastor objected to your choice of a substitute, for reasons of his own?"

"I should think that he had no right to do so, since the law or the Statutes entitle the assistant to a vacation."

"In this you are wrong."—The way the Bishop said it left the matter without further discussion. "Obey your pastor."

There were many other questions asked by the Bishop, which somehow brought out the force of various duties in the pastoral ministry. Thus, he wanted to know the difference between law and precept; between *commands,* statutes, directions, decisions and ecclesiastical sentences. In every case he dwelt on the duty of reverence and obedience as the foundation of order, harmony, clerical efficiency. "Obedience in the Church is never slavery; it is always voluntary, and, allied to the precept or spirit of humility, not to be separated from true charity."

When the Padre came back, after it was all over, the

Bishop said to him:

"I hope they have been taught to read their Breviary understandingly and reverently. I hold that reverence is the one virtue that for the cleric supplies all the other perfections and virtues of his state. There is broad an undue spirit of independence. It has caught the junior clergy. Reverence, not only for his superiors, but for his brethren, his people— each, a tabernacle of the soul and a child of God—I believe, is an essential pastoral quality of the efficient priest. It includes reverence for the sanctuary, for his own body, for every creature that bears the mark of God's design for man's use. If these young men daily recite the Hundred and Eighteenth Psalm thoughtfully, they can hardly forget the precept it embodies, which the Hebrews of old taught their children, of the presence of God, which means His Law."

With that, the Bishop took me from my velvet cushion and opened at Prime *In Die Dominica,* etc. Well, I felt fine, with the amethyst right on my page!

"Is it not a wonderful psalm, even in its literary workmanship? One can readily understand why it bears the name of the *Golden Alphabet.*"

The Padre only smiled, for there was nothing to say. He knew what the Bishop meant. The next day he brought the *Ordinandi* together, and explained to them the Hundred and Eighteenth Psalm, which they had to say every day. I have heard now, in my old age, that they don't say it as often, only once a week, because the reform of the Breviary called for a substitution of other psalms in the Little Hours for each day of the week, so that the clerics might recite the entire book of Psalms within the seven days.

That is all right, of course, because the Pope ordered it so. But I have noticed since the new practice has come into vogue with these "nova reformata" and "typica" counterfeits of the old Totum, the spirit of insubordination has considerably grown. Thank God, I am out of it, and on the shelf; for it would break my heart to get into the pockets of these new-fashioned coats one sees at baseball games and races. In fact, I could not do it—am too big and grand for such new-fangled notions of relaxation for the clergy! I confess that I had my suspicions all along about the "reformation" of the Breviary, because there is a bad sound to the word, at least since Luther started the business and people got to use it against the Church. But, then, it has really a different meaning in my ancestral city, Rome, and must be all right, whatever it does to lightheaded and short-coated clerics.

VIII. THE GOLDEN ALPHABET

The first thing those who were called to the priesthood orders saw as they entered the classroom, was a sort of chart which gave the skeleton of the Hundred and Eighteenth Psalm.

"This Psalm," said the Padre, "follows close upon the great Hallel series of prayers in the Jewish synagogue. It was the custom of the Hebrews to chant the six psalms bearing the title Hallelujah, as they went up to the temple processionally on the great days of the Pasch, Pentecost, Tabernacles and the feast of Dedication. In later times, during the Dispersion, they recited them, also on the day of the new moon.

"The special significance of these hymns in connection with the Eucharistic sacrifice became apparent on occasion of the Paschal celebration, which began on the eve of the fourteenth Nisan. This marks the service of the Last Supper on Holy Thursday. It is arranged as foreshadowing the Mass, and bridges over the ceremonial liturgy from the Old Law to the New Dispensation, as is shown in the following ritual of the Hebrew festival:

1. The head of the family prepares the sacrificial host, that is, the Paschal Lamb, together with the chalice of wine, unleavened bread and a vessel containing herbs (bitter).
2. Reads from the *Haggada* (Talmud) the account of the delivery of the Jews from the Egyptian bondage, and the institution of the Paschal celebration.
3. All the company chant the Hundred and Twelfth and Hundred and Thirteenth Psalms.
4. Act of Thanksgiving (Benediction).
5. Offering of the chalice with wine.
6. Partaking of the meal—which opens with
    (a) Washing of the hands
    (b) Breaking of Bread
    (c) Offering (Elevation) of the Bread
    (d) Eating (Communion)
    (e) Taking of the bitter herbs (Charoseth), and
    (f) Thanksgiving.
7. Drinking of the chalice, with blessing and chant of Psalms 114 to 117.
8. After the meal, the Hundred and Thirty-fifth Psalm—called the great Hallel—is taken up in unison by the assembly.

"The same order of prayer and offering was observed in the Eucharistic service of the Apostolic Church, as we glean from the so-called *Apostolic Constitutions.*

"It is to be noted that Psalm 114, which follows the

offering of the chalice—called the Hallel Chalice—contains prayers for

> the priest (10-12),
> converts (11-13),
> the children of the family (13-14),
> the destruction of heresy (8),—and
> a fruitful harvest (15-16).

"The next Psalm—115—expresses the *sacrificium laudis* in the taking of the chalice; while the two next psalms—116 and 117—are a prophetic echo of the Preface—Sursum corda, gratias agamus—of the Latin Mass."

And now the Padre turned to the Golden Alphabet, the Psalm that stood for the children of Israel, like the Thora itself, as the perfect expression of the Divine Law, and by the chanting of which he declared his readiness to observe it in all its phases.

Pointing to the chart he read out:

Verbum (Sermo)

1. Lex	6. Judicia
2. Mandatum (Prseceptum)	7. Eloquia
3. Justificationes (Justitia)	8. Via
4. Testimonia	9. Semita
5. Statuta	10. Veritas (fidelitas)

"These ten terms which are simply so many variations of the word *Verbum*, expressing different phases and degrees of the Divine Will or Law of God are, in one form or other, repeated in each stanza of the 176 verses of this Psalm. Yet, one would hardly notice the repetition. To the young Hebrew it became a lesson of respect for the Law in all its bearings upon practical life. Thus:

"Verbum (Sermo) Dabar—Logos—Word,

in verses: 9, 16, 17, 25, 28, 42, 49, 57, 65, 74, 81, 89, 101, 105, 107, 114, 130,139,147—indicates,

(a) the Divine Law and the word by which all things were created, and
(b) again the Word Incarnate, by which all men were redeemed, or created anew, after the fall. It is the law of the Spirit.

"Lex—Thora—Law,

in verses: 1, 18, 29, 34, 44, 51, 53, 55, 61, 70, 72, 77, 85, 92, 97, 109, 113, 126, 136, 142, 150, 153, 163, 165, 174—we have the natural law as delivered in the Decalogue, and the revealed Law as presented in the Gospel, the Law of sonship and charity.

"Mandatum (Præceptum)—Pequdim— Precepts,

in verses: 4, 15, 27, 40, 45, 56, 63, 69, 78, 87, 93, 94, 100, 104, 110, 128, 134, 141, 159, 168, 173—which signifies a precept of the patriarchal church, the synagogue or the Church of Christ, such as the law of circumcision, or abstinence, or the sacramental prescriptions.

"Justificationes (Justitia) Chuqim—Statutes,

in verses: 5, 8, 12, 16, 23, 26, 33, 48, 54, 64, 68, 71, 80, 83, 112, 117, 118, 124, 135, 145, 155, 171— These terms stand for Rules of conduct such as statutes and corrections, implying the law of equity or what is known as the 'golden rule.'

"Testimonia—Hedoth—Testimonies,

including civil and ecclesiastical regulations. The term recurs in verses: 2, 14, 22, 24, 31, 36, 46, 59, 79, 88, 95, 111, 119, 125, 129, 138, 144, 146, 152, 157, 167, 168.

"Statuta—Mitzoth—Commandments,

or agreements, vocational compacts, professional laws, as in verses: 6, 10, 19, 21, 32, 35, 47, 48, 60, 66, 73, 86, 96, 98, 115, 127, 131, 143, 151, 166, 172, 176.

"Judicia—Mispath—Judgments,

in verses: 7, 13, 20, 30, 39, 43, 52, 62, 75, 84, 91, 102, 106, 108, 120, 121, 137, 149, 156, 160, 164, 175—in which the law of what is fair, becoming and urbane in manner is expressed.

"Eloquia—Emer—Word,

expressing the dictates of conscience and repeated in verses: 11, 38, 41, 50, 58, 67, 76, 82, 103, 116, 123, 133, 140, 148, 154, 158, 162, 170.

"Via—Derek—Way,

the urgings of the soul, the spiritual word, the motive which becomes a law of action, expressed in verses: 1, 3, 5, 29, 30, 32, 33, 37, 59, 168.

"Semita—Orach—Path,

the law of traditional action—of custom, propriety,—as in verses, 9 and 15.

"Veritas—Tzedek—Righteousness,

the law which follows the standard of truth, right and fidelity, as in verses: 7, 40, 62, 75, 106, 121, 142, 164, 172."

It was high time for the Padre to stop; but he kept the students for a good half-hour after the bell had rung for recreation. We were late in our Vespers, which does not occur often, so I kept mum.

Sixth Part

I. THE TOTUM GETS A VACATION

AFTER the Ordinations I had a good rest. That is to say, I was not being perpetually dragged into the classroom to have my insides exposed and The Professor had other notions about sacramental rubrics and ceremonies which the Junior Theologians were studying, and when he took me in hand it was chiefly to say his prayers and get my advice as to how to behave. Indeed, I feel that the Padre had improved day by day so long as he used me as his monitor. Now and then I would give him a few hints, by making a sort of looking-glass out of the Second Nocturn. When he compared himself with the great saints, especially of the Confessor class, he knew that he might do a good deal more than he did, before he could make pretensions to be canonized, and that his Doctor title did not amount to much in presence of the Doctores Ecclesiæ with whom I consorted. Still, the Padre was doing pretty well, and never neglected me or treated me irreverently, as I have seen other Totums treated at times.

Things went on in the same way for a few months, and I was feeling very comfortable on my velvet prie-dieu, where I could disport my golden title *cum dignitate*.

But, alas for human frailty! A time came when I was to be put aside, though I was not at all old and had pretty well preserved my good looks.

The Bishop had made his visit "ad limina" to Rome, and when he returned, he brought a document for the Padre from the Pope. Well, such a fuss as they made, I never saw! He himself was not very much excited. But after a while I noticed that he blushed, not from anything wrong, but from all the purple millinery they put on him. I liked it well enough. To be seen in the hands of a Monsignor is befitting the dignity of a Totum. However, my pride and satisfaction were short-lived. The professors had arranged to celebrate his elevation to the rank of Notary Apostolic *ad instar,* whatever that means. Besides the dinner and speeches there was a formal reception, and presentation of things.—

I had been talking to him—Matins and Lauds—early in the afternoon, and he put me down with a sort of thump on the desk—not on the prie-dieu with the velvet cover—as if to say, "that's the last of you, old boy!" Yet, I could not have suspected that he really meant it. But trust even an old Padre! They all like novelties, and Russian leather, and a bit of personal convenience.

Well, that night the Padre came back into his library, where I was patiently waiting on the table. It was dark when he entered, and after fumbling about he pushed me aside to make room for some square box which I suspected must be books. What was my surprise and chagrin when the Padre, having turned on the light, deliberately took out of a black morocco case four new volumes bound in brown and gold, almost like his purple robes, and laid them beside me. I could plainly see on the front page the title *Breviarium Romanum—Editio Typica.* Here I was, who had done good service—almost, as I thought, made a saint of the old man—and now to be turned down; for that was clearly what was in store for me.

And so it happened. I could see how the Padre smiled at the upstart youngsters. It took four of them to make up for one of my size! Picking out the one that looked like a novel, he put it on the prie-dieu where *I* had been resting for years. The other three parts he locked in the case over his desk. Then he took *me*. I almost forgave him when he reverently kissed me. He removed some of the pictures and markers, and then, alas! chucked me under a shelf where he kept a lot of old fogies of books.

There I was buried alive for some time. One day a senior student came into the room with the Padre, who said to him: Look under there and you will probably find an old Totum which you can use until you get a set of your own—or keep it, if it serves your purpose. The young theologian was evidently pleased.

In this way I saw the light once more. He blew the dust off me and carried me to his room. It was different from the way I had been brought up. Hard boards instead of the fine prie-dieu with velvet! I was afraid the youngster might be wanting in respect for my dignity and age. But he was all right. When he showed me to his room-mate the latter said:

"Hello, Tim, where'dye get the Breviary?"

"The Dominie gave it to me."

"Why, it's only a Totum, though I wish he had given it to me. He is an old saint, and a book from him is worth a mine of gold."

"That's so," said Timothy, "I am going to keep it, and try to be a good boy.

"Now, Timothy Hasson, or "Tim," as he was called by his classmates, was an Irish student. He had studied his philosophy at Louvain, where the Bishop, visiting the Seminary, had adopted him for the American mission because they had more priests in Limerick than were needed there. He was to be ordained shortly and the Bishop was rather fond of him, for he was a Limerick man himself. But, for that matter, everybody liked Tim, who was good-natured and good at his studies.

Well, with Tim I had to go to class once more. But there was now another professor of liturgy. He was a young man. They said he could play the organ and the flute, and wrote poetry. The Padre, being a monsignor, it was, I suppose, beneath his dignity to go regularly to class.

II. NEW LIFE AND HEBREW MUSIC

The first time Tim took me into class, they discussed the hymns of the different Offices. All the Ambrosian and Gregorian hymns were taken up in regular order. Then the canticles. It was quite interesting, for the Professor went over the origin, history and peculiar art of each composition. It put new life into my old pages, for poetry makes one young, they say.

The way the new Professor spoke, it was evident he had been a pupil of the Padre. He praised the Totum, and made the students realize that I was joyous company and not a burden, so long as there was no misunderstanding between us. To prove his point he began with the *Canticles,* and showed them how Moses was a poet and wrote two beautiful hymns for the Totum, just as he wrote the Law for the Israelites:

1. *First Canticle of Moses.*[7] Begins with the words *Cantemus Domino: gloriose enim magnificatus est.* It was a union of the sentiments such as you find in the Ambrosian *Te Deum* and in the *Magnificat.* In it Moses gives thanks for the delivery of the Jewish people after their flight from Egypt and their wonderful passage

---

[7] Ex. 15:1-18.

through the Red Sea. The chant is a dramatic piece, and has furnished the inspiration for the oratorical symphony of *Moses in Egypt* by Handel; and later for the work of Rossini, *Israel in Egypt*. The nineteenth verse, "Ingressus est enim eques Pharao cum curribus et equitibus ejus in mare, et reduxit super eos Dominus aquas maris: filii autem Israel ambulaverunt per siccum in medio ejus," did not belong, the Padre said, to the original composition. It was an addition of a later writer, who adapted the canticle to the commemoration service of thanksgiving for the delivery from bondage, which was annually held in the temple at Jerusalem, and later in the synagogues of the dispersed tribes.

The significance of the Canticle lies in its application to the sacraments of Baptism and the Holy Eucharist, in which the delivery from the enemy through the saving waters of regeneration and the miraculous feeding in the desert are commemorated. Hence, it has always been recited on Thursday, the day of the week which is consecrated to the institution of the Blessed Sacrament.—But there is another piece composed by Moses and chanted in the Canonical Office. It is called the

2. *Second Canticle of Moses*,[8] and begins *Audite coeli, quæ loquor*. It is the swan-song of the great liberator, when on the eve of his death he called together the Elders of his people, as he looked from the mountain of Moab across the Jordan, which separated them from the Promised Land of Cana, and gave them his last injunctions to remain faithful to the God of their Fathers who had brought them hither. He calls on the heavens and on all the earth to hear him. And, in truth, the sound

---

[8] Deut. 32:1-42.

of his voice has gone to the ends of the earth and reechoes from the heavens to this day. The chant, after a brief intonation, like an antiphon, recalls the mercies of God, His promises to His people and His power to punish and to save. It ends with an Epilogue, or Epiphone, in which the aged prophet addresses the nations of the earth, bidding them to heed the call of the elect Church of God, and not to destroy or persecute it:

> Laudate Gentes, populum ejus
> Quia sanguinem servorum suorum ulciscetur,
> Et vindictam retribuet in hostes eorum;
> Et propitus erit terræ populi sui.

It is a Sabbath chant of gratitude and used in the Divine Office accordingly.

Of the seventeen Canticles in the Totum, the remaining Old Testament chants belong to the period of the different captivities; they are in part prophetic. From Isaiah we have two:

3. *Cantica Isaiæ.*[9] The first of these begins *Confitebor tibi, Domine.* It is a thanksgiving ode for the delivery of the Israelites from the attack of the Assyrians, and has a Messianic note of hope in the coming of Christ. "Haurietis aquas in gaudio de fontibus Salvatoris, et dicetis in die illa: Confitemini Domino . . . quoniam magnifice fecit; annunciate hoc in universa terra."—The second song from the same prophet is "Vere tu es Deus absconditus,"[10] Thou art, O Lord, truly a hidden God! It announces the immediate delivery of Israel from the foreign yoke and the rebuilding of the temple under Cyrus. In a wider sense, it predicts the establishment of the Church of Christ and His abiding presence in the

---

[9] Is. 12:1-6.

[10] Is. 45:15-26.

Mystery of the Altar.

4. *Jeremias.* Another canticle of prophetic import is inserted in the Office for Thursday. It is the appeal of Jeremias, during the captivity of Babylon, to his fellow exiles to trust in the Lord, who will lead His people back to peace in its home country. "Audite verbum Domini, Gentes, et annunciate in insulis quae procul sunt."[11] It applies in particular to the promises of the permanent presence of Christ with His Church in the Holy Eucharist, and His pastoral care of the flock:

"Custodiet eum (Israel) sicut pastor gregem suum.... Et venient et laudabunt in monte Sion, et confluent ad bona Domini.

"Super frumento et vino.... Eritque anima eorum quasi hortus irriguus et ultra non esurient.

"Tunc lætabitur virgo in choro, juvenes et senes simul. ...

"Et inebriabo animam sacerdotum pinguedine, et populus meus bonis meis adimplebitur."

Frequently the note of joy and gratitude is introduced in the psalms of the penitential season, to raise the heart with hope amid sorrow and affliction, or to point out that sacrifice is rendered sweet through the love with which it is being offered, despite the apparent hardships. Of this character are the

5. *Cantica Trium Puerorum, of which we* have two in the Canonical Hours. The first of these is the chant of Ananias, Azarias and Misael when, having refused to adore the statue erected by Nabuchodonosor, they were cast into the furnace to be burnt. They invite the elements and all nature to praise God; and the destructive

---

[11] Jer. 31:10-14.

flames become to them a solace and joy. The canticle forms the chief part of the priestly thanksgiving after Mass, and is embodied in the Sunday Office. It belongs to the Book of Daniel[12] but is not found in the present Hebrew Bible. St. Jerome translated it from the Greek text. Theodotion and the Septuagint also have it. The second Canticle is likewise a hymn of praise, forming part of the same account in Daniel; it is recited separately in the Sunday Office of Lent. Next we have a unique hymn by

6. *David.* Whilst the greater number of the song-meditations contained in the Psalter owe their origin to David, there is a hymn found in the Book of Chronicles[13] not counted among the Psalms, which is attributed to him by the sacred historian. It is the *Benedictus* of the Old Law, and was composed by the King when, nearing the end of his life, he had arranged for the building of the temple by his son Solomon. The people had been invited to bring their gifts to the King, that they might be consecrated, together with the treasures gathered by him during his reign, for the future building of the sanctuary. The crowds of joyous Israelites came from all parts, and as the aged sovereign looked out upon the multitude, the Divine Spirit awakened in him this chant of gratitude:

> Benedictus es, Domine,
> Deus Israel Patris nostri, ab æterno in æternum.
> Tua et Domine, magnificentia,
> Et potentia, et gloria. . . .
> Nunc igitur, Deus noster,
> Confitemur tibi, et laudamus Nomen tuum inclytum.

---

[12] 3:57-90.

[13] I Paralip, 29:10-13.

7. *Ezechias.* Another King of later time, while the prophet Isaiah was still living, has left us a canticle of thanksgiving for his delivery from a serious illness. Ezechias describes his feelings in face of death, and his prayer. The prophet Isaiah is called to pray, and announces to the King his recovery. The last part is a chant of gratitude poured from the royal heart. It belongs to the Office of the Dead, and expresses the Christian sentiment—*vita non tollitur sed mutatur.*

8. *Habacuc.* Of the Minor Prophets the Breviary has a song of lament by Habacuc[14] in which a vivid picture is drawn of the Divine Judgments. The immediate occasion of the prophecy is God's wrath against the Chaldeans. Its purpose in the Divine Office is to excite sorrow for sin through fear of the Judgment at the hour of death.

9. *Tobias and Judith.* There are two canticles of earlier date—that of the elder Tobias[15] and another of Judith.[16] The former is an expression of gratitude for the graces of the faith and mercy of Jehovah amid the captivity, which Tobias openly avers is deserved by himself and his people for their neglect to observe the Divine law. The other is a chant of exultant joy over the delivery of the Jewish people from the tyranny of the Assyrian Holofernes by the hand of a woman, at a time when the priests and elders were ready to surrender their people to the invader. Its keynote of admonition is: Trust in God.

10. *Jesus Ben Sirach.* The young professor said that Ben Sirach was a Jewish priest of Jerusalem who collaborated with the seventy-two rabbis, called to Alexandria by King Ptolemy to translate the Hebrew

---

[14] 3:1-10.

[15] 13:1-10.

[16] 16:15-21.

Thora into Greek (Septuagint version). After completing this work he returned to Jerusalem and wrote his famous Wisdom treatise, known as the Book of *Ecclesiasticus*, in Hebrew. It was later translated into Greek by a young relation of his. From this work a Latin version was made for the Catholic Vulgate. Recently, I hear, fragments of the original Hebrew text have been discovered. It is a wonderful book, and inspired, although Jews and Protestants do not admit this. But the Catholic Church has always held it to be so, and draws many lessons from it for the Preacher, from which the book is named in the Greek tongue. It contains all kinds of instructions for the guidance of the individual and the direction of the family, the education of children, the government of the state and the ruling of the Church. In the thirty-sixth chapter the writer suddenly interrupts his reflections and utters a prayer for the safety and guidance of the Church of Jerusalem. I don't think the Padre would agree to all the young professor said about Ben Sirach. But the book which bears his name is all right. This particular prayer has been styled the *Canticle of Ecclesiasticus* and is repeated by the priest in the ferial Office of Saturday.

11. *Zachary and Simeon.* Whilst the canticle *Benedictus*, of Zachary, is a hymn of thanksgiving on the part of the Aaronic priest, it is also an outline of the priestly life in Christ. The image of the Redeemer is drawn as bringing salvation and joy to men who are held captive in sin. He comes that He may bring mercy and liberty of spirit and peace. Then follows the appeal to the child John—the future precursor. "And thou, His herald, His ambassador, shalt go before Him to prepare His way,

    (a) to give the knowledge of salvation unto His people;
    (b) to remit their sins;
    (c) to enlighten those who are in darkness and sit in the

NEW LIFE AND HEBREW MUSIC 161

shadow of death; and
(d) to direct our steps in the ways of peace."

To the fulfilment of this mission in the Baptist, as the Forerunner of Christ, Simeon next bears witness. At the coming of the Savior to the Temple, the venerable priest welcomes the Holy Child and Its Mother, and then bids farewell to the Old-Testament world by the words

> Nunc dimittis, Domine,
> servum tuum in pace.

But the most important and beautiful of all the Canticles in the Breviary are

12. *The Chant of Hannah (Anna) and the Magnificat of Our Blessed Lady.* When Our Blessed Lady had received the message of the archangel Gabriel, and felt the Holy Child resting under her Immaculate Heart, she arose and quickly went to visit her cousin Elizabeth, that she might learn her duties as Mother. It was her first Holy Communion, with the Incarnate Word in her bosom as Its tabernacle. On the journey Our Lady meditated, it appears, on the life of a saintly matron a thousand years earlier. Hannah (Anna) wife of Eleana, and mother of Samuel, the future High-priest, who, on having received the grace of an unexpected and blessed maternity, rendered thanks to God in a canticle, became a model of Hebrew mothers. Her chant of gratitude is preserved among the inspired writings in the Book of Kings.[17] This beautiful song must have been in the mind of Mary, for she repeats its chief thoughts, only adding to the sweetness of its melody by the association of a Redeemer. It re-echoes portions of the psalter of David and other

---

[17] I Kings 2:1-10.

inspired singers, but the words of both Magnificats are in parts almost identical:

Hannah (Anna)	*Maria*
Exultavit cor meum in Domino et exaltatum est cornu meum in Deo meo.	Et exultavit spiritus meus in Deo salutari meo.
Repleti prius, pro panibus se locaverunt; et famelici saturati sunt.	Esurientes implevit bonis, et divites dimisit inanes,
Dominus pauperem facit et ditat, humiliat et sublevat.	Fecit potentiam in brachio suo. . . .
Suscitat de pulvere egenum, et de stercore elevat pauperem,	Deposuit potentes de sede, et exaltavit humiles;
Ut sedeat cum principibus. . . .Dominus judicabit fines terræ . . .et sublimabit cornu Christi sui.	Suscepit Israel puerum suum, recordatus misericordiæ suæ. Sicut locutus est ad patres nostros, Abraham et semini ejus in sæcula.

The students seemed to like the young Professor, and the way he explained my musical contents. Still, I was glad when the classes were over, because I remembered the horrid examinations. Sure enough, they came at the end of the term. This time the questions were more reasonable, and the examiners seemed to be easily satisfied. Perhaps they didn't know as much about the Canticles and chant as the Professor, who was a musical doctor, and who pointed out for them the subject matter, which mainly comprised questions about the poetry of the Breviary. He seemed to have the hymns and their authors at his fingers' ends, and I felt quite elated when he showed them what a learned company I frequented. They pretended, of course, to know all about the composers of the hymns.

There was Sedulius, for instance, who had written the hymns *A solis ortus cardine* for Christmas and the *Crudelis Herodes, Deum*— which the correctors of Pope Urban VIII changed from the original *Hostis Herodes impie*. This is the hymn chanted at Vespers of the Epiphany.

They got through their task in short order, because there were only a few deacons to be promoted. It was all over before dinner. But I must tell you more about the hymns some other time, because my young master wants to recite his Vespers now.

III. Deacon Tim Wants to Know More about the Christian Poets

Somehow, the examinations did not satisfy Deacon Tim Hasson, although the candidates were passed "summa cum laude." During the following class days before the ordination, he asked the Professor for more particulars about the hymns. The Professor liked Tim, who was something of a poet himself. He also knew that, and knew that the Padre had given him me, the Totum, because young Hasson was a close student, likely to develop a talent for writing. The Padre had great respect for young men who cultivated the gift of composition. He used to say to the students in his class:

"Write, write! cultivate the habit constantly. Copy everything that strikes you in your reading as particularly beautiful or useful. These thoughts, put on paper, not only remain in your memory and serve you as illustration in your later work of preaching, but they crystallize in the soul and help you to build up character. Moreover, they increase your opportunities for attracting others to the truth, by generating the habit of expressing yourselves beautifully in conversing with men."

The Professor must have told the Padre about Tim's predilection, with the result that when, before the Retreat, the *ordinandi* received their final instructions from the Monsignor, he talked about the hymns, instead of how they should behave when they got their appointments as assistants after ordination.

"There is a great deal of dogmatic, moral and pastoral instruction," he said to the young men, "to be found in the hymns of the Breviary. You begin with those of Advent:

> Creator alme siderum,
> Æterna lux credentium,
> Jesu Redemptor omnium,
> Intende votis supplicum.

You notice how the opening stanzas of the Vesper hymn unfold the sentiment of the season, which is carried on through the hymn of Matins.

> Verbum supernum prodiens
> E Patris æterni sinu,
> Qui natus orbi subvenis
> Labente cursu temporis.

The thought is continued through Lauds, in which the final note of the Advent-promise is sounded in the verses

> En Agnus ad nos mittitur

THE CHRISTIAN POETS 165

> Laxare gratis debitum:
> Omnes simul cum lacrimis
> Precemur indulgentiam."

These, he said, were compositions of probably the fifth century. The style was that of St. Ambrose; though the words had been changed in parts so as to bring them in line with the metric requirements of the classicists. This was done by the direction of Urban VIII.

The theme is maintained in the Christmas hymns which at Vespers introduce the Holy Child with a cradle song:

> Jesu Redemptor omnium,
> Quem lucis ante originem
> Parem Paternæ gloriæ
> Pater supremus edidit.

But at Lauds a new feature is added in a hymn by the priest-poet Sedulius, who lived about the time of St. Ambrose or a little later. He wrote very beautifully about the Creation and the great events of the Old and New Testaments. Among other things he composed a sort of golden Alphabet, somewhat in the style of the Hundred and Eighteenth Psalm. It is usually called the *Abecedarian* Ode. Most of it he gave to the Totum as a sort of Christmas present. Here it is, with a nice English translation for the students, so that the Professor need not always lug me into the classroom. He himself told them that if they read these hymns in English while they follow their studies, it helps them afterward in their devotion when they recite them in Latin from my pages for prayer. The English version is by a scholarly Cambridge man, Dr. John Mason Neale, who was a great friend of the Totum. He only died in 1866, so that I can say I knew him almost personally.

The Padre gave the Alphabetical form as it occurs in the Offices of Christmas and Epiphany. But please pay attention to the irregularities introduced by the hymn critics who, whilst they could never have written such a beautiful hymn themselves, wanted to improve the classical style of Sedulius—the Lord forgive them! It's all right, though, because the Pope approved it. Truly, it is not a matter of infallibility; still, we have to keep step and rhythm in the procession; otherwise there would be nothing but disorder, and all our hymn-singing would not please God, no matter how well written it might be.

For Christmas

A solis ortus cardine Ad usque terræ limitem, Christum canamus Principem, Natum Maria Virgine.	From lands that see the sun arise, To earth's remotest boundaries, The Virgin - Born today we sing, The Son of Mary, Christ the King.
Beatus Auctor sæculi, Servile corpus induit: Ut carne carnem liberans, Ne perderet quos condidit.	Blest Author of this earthly frame, To take a servant's form He came, That, liberating flesh by flesh, Whom He had made might live afresh.
Castæ parentis viscera Cœlestis intrat gratia: Venter puellæ bajulat	In that chaste parent's holy womb

THE CHRISTIAN POETS

Secreta, quæ non noverat.	Celestial grace has found its home; And she, as earthly bride unknown, Yet calls that Offspring blest her own.
Domus pudici pectoris Templum repente fit Dei: Intacta nesciens virum, Concepit alvo Filium.	The mansion of the modest breast Becomes a shrine where God shall rest: The pure and undefiled one, Conceived in her womb the Son.

Well, Sedulius did not write the last verse just that way. He said *Verbo concepit Filium* instead of *Concepit alvo Filium.* But the poetical tinkers (of course I don't want to be disrespectful to the Holy Father, since he let it go) who "reformed" the hymn thought that a spondee in the first foot of an iambic dimeter, would not be good form.

Having once begun to criticize, they kept right on, and in the next stanza changed *Enixa est puerpera* to *Enititur puerpera* and *Clausus Joannes senserat* to *Baptista clausum senserat.* Anybody can see that Sedulius was right in using the name John, which means "Grace of God," rather than Baptist, which reminds one of the Dunkers, and of one Roger Williams who would not let anyone get to heaven except through a swimming pool. That would keep most of the little children out of Paradise, or else you would have to drown them. It was all right in the early days when you had to make sure that a pagan or a Jew really would be baptized, for they were a hard lot in the beginning and only softened by the grace of the sacraments, gradually, as they were brought up in the Church.

The new forms run this way:

Enititur puerpera	That Son, that Royal Son,
Quem Gabriel prædixerat	she bore,
Quem ventre Matris gestiens,	Whom Gabriel's voice had told afore;
Baptista clausum senserat.	Whom, in His Mother yet concealed,
	The infant Baptist had revealed.
Fœno jacere pertulit:	The manger and the straw He bore,
Præsepe non abhorruit:	
Et lacte modico pastus est,	The cradle did He not abhor;
Per quem nec ales esurit.	By milk, in infant portions, fed,
	Who gives e'en fowls their daily bread.
Gaudet chorus Cœlestium,	The heavenly chorus filled the sly,
Et Angeli canunt Deo;	
Palamque fit pastoribus	The Angels sang to God on high,
Pastor, Creator omnium.	
	What time to shepherds watching lone,
	They made creation's Shepherd known.

These seven stanzas, beginning with A down to G, and adding the Doxology *Jesu, tibi sit gloria*, complete the Lauds of Christmas Day.

But on the eve of Epiphany we take up the continuation of the same hymn. The Vesper chant completes the prophetic picture of the Christ who appears on earth. Sedulius wrote it all out in full, making twenty-three stanzas, each beginning with one of the successive letters of the alphabet, as I have already said. His idea was to remind us that this Holy Child was the Alpha and Omega of all blessings on earth, and that the knowledge of the Christ meant the wisdom of all earthly science.

Here again the Humanist correctors interfered. Sedulius wrote, beginning with the next letter *H*:

> Hostis Herodes impie,
> Christum venire quid times!

But they could not brook the idea that the initial foot of an iambic dimeter should begin with a trochee. They forgot that the letter *H* might be used as a consonant and prolong the final syllable of the first foot, and that *Herodes* could be emphasized at the end, a thing which Fortunatus and other poets, as good as the Urban people, did repeatedly. So they destroyed the alphabetical sequence, dropping the *H* and making me sing:

Crudelis Herodes, Deum	Why, impious Herod,
Regem venire quid times?	vainly fear
Non eripit mortalia,	That Christ the Savior
Qui regna dat cœlestia.	cometh here?
	He takes no earthly realms away
	Who gives the crown that lasts for aye.

After that they went on with Sedulius, following the A-B-C order:

Ibant Magi, quam viderant,	To greet His birth the Wise Men went,
Stellam sequentes præviam:	Led by the star before them sent;
Lumen requirunt lumine:	Called on by light, towards Light they pressed,
Deum fatentur munere.	And by their gifts their God confessed.

Here again they suppressed the letter *K*, which the Homan poet had inserted, beginning the verse *Katerva Matrum;* and they also omitted the letter *M* where Sedulius had the line *Miraculis dedit,* in which the slaughter of the Innocents is described. They did not want to repeat the idea belonging to the feast of the Holy Innocents, and for which Prudentius furnishes a separate hymn. One can forgive them that, though it spoils the alphabet. The verses of Prudentius are really charming. You remember the opening salutation:

> Salvete, flores martyrum,
> Quos lucis ipso in limine
> Christi insecutor sustulit,
> Ceu turbo nascentes rosas.

We must return to Sedulius, however, who continues:

Lavacra puri gurgitis	In holy Jordan's purest wave
Cœlestis Agnus attigit:	The heavenly Lamb
Peccata, quæ non detulit,	

Nos abluendo sustulit.	vouchsafed to lave; That He to whom was sin unknown, Might cleanse His people from their own.
Novum genus potentiæ: Aquæ rubescunt hydriæ, Vinumque jussa fundere, Mutavit unda originem.	New miracle of power Divine; The water reddens into wine He spake the word and poured the wave In other streams than nature gave.

That was the only hymn which the new Professor treated in detail. His chief purpose was, as he told the students, to give them a sample of the beautiful things and the music that were in the Totum. He said hoped they would take up the study of the other hymns at their first opportunity after ordination, because their whole education in the Seminary had been preparing them for such work.

Before the ordination to the priesthood, which took place at the end of the term, the Padre came again into the class on several occasions. They had to remember that he was now a monsignor, with purple rabbi and a red lining to his soutane. Once or twice he had the *Pars Verna* in his hand while he spoke to the theologians. I think Timothy Hasson, who had been made a Reverend Deacon, knew very well that the Totum he had before him was much more important and perfect than the pretentious *Pars* which the Padre carried. He was very proud of me, and often said that he would not part with his Totum for all the Breviaries and their gold and leather liveries. He knew, as well as myself that old men, like the Padre, could not so easily carry a Totum, because of their age and growing infirmity; but, after all, the proper Breviary was the Totum, even if you had to take it apart for the sake of comfort.

On one occasion the Monsignor spoke of the beautiful poetry of the Psalms. Later he returned to the hymns, and told the *ordinandi* to look them up in the order of the feasts on which they occurred. Most of them were masterpieces, he said, of dogmatic teaching as well as poetry of a high order. All the great Fathers and theologians of the Church were represented in the course of the year. He mentioned in particular among the Fathers of the early Church: *St. Ambrose* as the author of such beautiful hymns as

> Æterna Christi munera
> Apostolorum gloriam
> Palmas et hymnos debitos
> Lætis canamus mentibus.

These verses, he told them, were being chanted at Matins of the Apostles' feasts. They had been adopted, in slightly changed form, for the feast of several martyrs. I could easily see that the Padre did not approve the changes made in the Ambrosian hymns by the correctors of Urban VIII. They changed nearly all the chants for the ferial Offices, though they respected the main thought and the doctrinal purpose, which are in every case those of the great Bishop of Milan.

St. Gregory is another of the Patristic authors who composed a number of beautiful hymns, such as the

Matin song

> Primo die, quo Trinitas
> Beata mundum condidit,
> Vel quo resurgens Conditor
> Nos, morte victa, liberat.

I should have mentioned before these, St. Hilary of Poitiers, of whom St. Isidore of Seville writes:

> "Hymnorum carmine floruit primus."

He is author of the lines sung at Lauds on Pentecost Sunday.

> Beata nobis gaudia
> Anni reduxit orbita,
> Cum Spiritus Paraclitus
> Illapsus est Apostolis.

That is the text as I have it, but the Padre said that St. Hilary wrote the last line this way:

> *Effulsit in discipulos*

which is more exact historically. But, then, Pope Urban VIII preferred the change. He had got some hymns of his own in the Totum also, which are, I must say, models of classical correctness. Here is a sample on the feast of St. Martina, Virgin and Martyr, whose body was recovered in a tomb at the foot of the Capitol in Rome during his Pontificate. This event caused a special devotion to the saint, and the Pope himself composed the three hymns in her honor for the feast on the 30th of January.

Martinæ celebri plaudite nomini
Cives Romulei, plaudite gloriæ:
Insignem meritis dicite Virginem,
Christi dicite Martyrem.

You notice the strictly classical style of the asclepiadic strophe.

She is not the only saint for whom Pope Urban VIII had a special devotion. He canonized St. Elizabeth of Portugal, niece of St. Elizabeth of Hungary, and on the occasion composed two hymns in her honor. The first of these is unique in the hymnody of the Breviary. It is written in the archiloquian style of the Horatian odes, but not a mere imitation. The strophe consists of three verses; the first an iambic trimeter, six feet; a dactylic trimeter catalectic; and an iambic dimeter:

Domare cordis impetus Elizabeth
Fortis inopsque Deo
Servire regno prætulit.

The second is an iambic trimeter, and reads very smoothly, attending rather to quantity than to accent.

Opes, decusque regium reliqueras
Elizabeth, Deidicata numini:
Recepta nunc bearis inter Angelos;
Libens ab hostium tuere nos dolis.

Præi, viamque dux salutis indica:
Sequemur. O sit una mens fidelium,
Odor bonus sit omnis actio, tuis
Id innuit rosis operta caritas.

THE CHRISTIAN POETS 175

But a matchless piece of prayerful poesy is the hymn which this Pontiff genius composed for the Office of St. Theresa. It was inserted in the Roman Totum in 1629.

> Regis superni nuntia
> Domum paternam deseris,
> Terris Teresa barbaris
> Christum datura, aut sanguinem.
>
> Sed te manet suavior
> Mors, pœna poscit dulcior:
> Divini amoris cuspide
> In vulnus icta concides.
>
> O caritatis victima!
> Tu corda nostra concrema,
> Tibique gentes creditas
> Averni ab igne libera.

There are other hymns by St. Fortunatus and by St. Bernard and Rabanus Maurus. The latter was a great lover of St. Michael and wrote the fine sapphic ode

> Christe Sanctorum decus Angelorum,
> Rector humani generis et Auctor
> Nobis æternum tribue benignus
> Scandere cœlum.

Perhaps it was he too who wrote the hymn for confessors and bishops: *Iste confessor Domini colentes* or (sacratus), though that is not at all certain. There were other priests and monks who wrote fine poetry. The Totum has some by Blessed Hermannus Contractus and St. Thomas of Aquin who sang quite as beautifully as Prudentius himself. And I almost forgot Fra Jacopone, who gave us the touching *Stabat Mater Dolorosa*.

Occasionally I got hymns inspired by one saint and written by another. One such is the royal chant of the

> Vexilla Regis prodeunt,
> Fulget crucis mysterium,
> Qua Vita mortem pertulit,
> Et morte vitam protulit.

This was written by St. Fortunatus at the request of St. Radegonda, who had obtained a relic of the true cross from the Empress Sophia, and wanted a processional hymn to mark its reception. Later St. Francis de Sales made a fine French translation of the same which is a favorite of the nuns of the Visitation.

But I cannot remember all that the Padre told them about these symphonies. He just shut me up when he spoke about the hymns which Pope Leo XIII, who had given him the title of Monsignor, had recently composed. I don't recognize them, for the Totum of the fine old days sticks to the earlier traditions, and though I have great reverence for the Pope, still he is not infallible when he makes poetry, no matter how good it is.

IV. The Last "Drop" and the Totum Is Pensioned

The time came at last when the Reverend Deacon Timothy Hasson was called to the sacred priesthood. It was a great day. He got a lot of presents, and also a new set of Breviaries— the editio Typica. But, God bless him; he just looked at the fancy volumes, and then put them on the bureau with his other presents. He has stuck to the Totum all these years, except occasionally when he had to make a show. He said he liked me because I had been given to him by the Padre. But I think he liked me anyhow, until I had that unfortunate fall from the balcony, while he went on the fishing trip with Father O'More, and the book-binder ruined my complexion, about which I told you at the beginning.

FINIS

GLOSSARY

Ad limina (Lat. "to the threshold")—a term in ecclesiastical language to designate the periodical visit of bishops to Rome in order to give an account of their administration and state of the diocese. Since A.D. 743, when these visits were made official, they include a pilgrimage to the tombs of the Apostles Peter and Paul, whence the expression.

Alexandrine Text—a Greek version of the Old Testament made at Alexandria (Egypt) during the third century before Christ.

Antiphonary of Bangor—a book of antiphons or responsive chants used by the monks of the monastery of Bangor (Ulster) during the seventh century.

Apocrypha—Biblical writings whose inspiration was at times disputed. Also applied to spurious imitations of Scripture claimed as inspired and as belonging to the Canon or authorized collection of biblical books.

Apostolic Constitutions—an unofficial collection of Church ordinances attributed to the Apostles, but bearing marks of a later date (IV cent.).

Athanasian Creed—a summary of Catholic doctrine, explained by St. Athanasius (IV cent.) To emphasize the belief in the Holy Trinity it was made a part of the regular Sunday Office since the IX century.

Bollandists—a company of Jesuit scholars who under the initiative of Jean Bollandus, S.J., undertook in 1612 to edit a critical history of saints; continued since then under the title of *Acta Sanctorum*.

Butler, Alban—(1710-1773) edited a series of Lives of Saints in English, which was continued by his nephew Charles Butler, down to 1823.

Bull—an official letter or document issued by the Pope, which takes its name from the leaden seal (Lat. *bulla*) appended for its authentication.

Canonical Hours—the prayers assigned by the canons, or rules, of the Church to certain hours when the clergy or Religious assembled to recite them in common.

Canon Law—a digest of the doctrinal and disciplinary laws of the Church.

Canon of St. Gregory—the formula of the solemn part of the Mass prescribed originally by St. Gregory (d. 604).

Capitulum—a short reading of parts of Holy Scripture, which occurs in the recitation of the Canonical Hours.

Commune Sanctorum—the part of the Canonical Office in which are the psalms, hymns and prayers, to be recited on the feasts of saints, and belonging to certain groups such as martyrs, confessors, virgins, etc.

Compline—the last (seventh) of the Canonical Hours, completing the daily recitation of the Office-prayers. It is the official night-prayer of the Church.

Con-non-Pon.—an abbreviation for *Confessor non Pontifex* designating a confessor saint in the Canonical Office who was not a bishop.

Council of Trent—a universal assembly of the Catholic hierarchy the principal sessions of which were held between 1545 and 1563, in the city of Trent (Austria-Hungary), to define Catholic doctrines questioned by the so-called Reformation, and to re-enact laws of ecclesiastical discipline under the authority of the Church. Political reasons urged the holding of the Council in Germany rather than at Rome.

Cycle, ecclesiastical—the period or round of festal celebrations in the Church during the year, beginning

GLOSSARY

with Advent.

Cyclus Epactorum—the period or number of days indicating the excess of the solar year over twelve lunar months; generally about eleven days.

Divine Office—the service of prayer in the Church officially determined by the Canonical Hours of the Breviary.

Dominical Letter—(see *Litteræ Dominicales*).

Doxology—the concluding form of praise or prayer in the liturgical services, such as the *Gloria Patri* with which the different psalms and orations conclude.

Egyptian Text—the text of the Greek translation of the Old Testament made in Egypt (Alexandria) for the exiled Jews, who did not speak Hebrew.

Enoch (Henoch)—the seventh patriarch before Noe, and father of Methusalem, believed to have been bodily taken into heaven owing to his piety. According to the belief of the Christian Fathers he will reappear with Eli in the last days to preach repentance.

Epact *(see* Cyclus Epactorum).

Ferverino—a short sermon produced from the fervor of the heart.

Gallican Psalter—a revision of the Latin Psalms made by St. Jerome and first adopted by the bishops in Gaul for the Offices of the Church.

Golden Alphabet—the 118th Psalm, so called because in the Hebrew the successive verses, in groups of eight, follow the order of the Alphabet. Since the Psalm inculcates the observance of the Law of God, the alphabetical order was supposed to help the memory, and was taught to the young as the "Golden Alphabet."

Golden Letter—(see *Litteræ Aureæ*).

Hexapla (Greek "sixfold")—an edition of the Bible in six versions. It is the particular name for a collation of six text forms of the Old Testament made by Origen, which gives in six parallel columns the Hebrew, its pronunciation in Greek letters, and four different Greek versions extant at his time.

Homily—a brief discourse explaining Scriptural passages.

Itala—a Latin version of the Bible in use before St. Jerome made his Latin translation called the Vulgate. It was probably made in Italy, but became popular in the Church of North Africa where it was known as *Itala*.

Jahweh (Jehovah)—Hebrew for "Lord" applied to God.

King James Version—an English translation of the Bible, authorized by King James of England for the Protestant churches (1611).

Lauds—the canonical prayers of Praise, the Hour which follows immediately on the Matins, or morning Office; recited after midnight, unless anticipated by privilege.

Lectio brevis—a short reading from Scripture or from the writings of the Fathers, introduced in the Hour of Prime.

Litteræ Aureæ (Golden Letters)—designating the number of the Paschal full-moon in successive years. It was indicated in the ancient MS. kalendars in letters of gold.

Litteræ Dominicales—the first seven letters of the Alphabet used respectively to mark the Sundays in the kalendar.

Little Chapter (see *Capitulum*)—like *lectio brevis*, a short reading from Scripture introduced during canonical prayer.

Little Hours—the four Hours of Prime, Terce, Sext and None, because they are brief.

Martyrology—an official record of the acts of martyrs,

and of the celebration of feasts arranged according to the days of the year.

Matins—the morning Office of the Church, consisting of three Nocturns, or divisions of the night watches.

Milanese Liturgy—the church-service-of the city and diocese of Milan. Its ritual dates from the time of St. Ambrose and is retained by privilege although it differs from the Roman.

Mizmor—Hebr. for *Psalm* or musical meditation.

Nocturn—Night Hour, applied to parts of the Matin service.

None—Ninth Hour, name of one of the four Little Hours.

Notary Apostolic—originally the title of a Roman official, who was appointed to keep record of the acts of martyrs in the Church. At present it designates the function of a member of the Roman Chancery. The addition *ad instar* indicates that the office is honorary.

Ordo—is the official directory to guide those who recite the Canonical Office in the observance of the feasts and commemorations, which also affect the manner of celebrating Mass.

Pars Æstiva—Part of the Breviary or Canonical Office which pertains to the summer season, as

Pars Autumnalis—covers the Offices of autumn,

Pars Hiemalis—those of the winter term, and

Pars Verna—those of spring.

Pontifical Mass—a Mass celebrated solemnly by a bishop.

Prime—the first of the Little Hours in the daily canonical prayer.

Proprium de Tempore—that part of the Divine Office in the Breviary which marks the regular seasons of the ecclesiastical year, such as Advent, Lent, etc., apart from the special feasts of saints, etc.

Proprium Sanctorum—that part of the Divine Office in the Breviary which notes the succession of special feasts of saints, etc.

Psalterium—a collection of the psalms recited in the regular Office.

Responsoriale of Gregory I—a liturgical guide for chanting the responses of the Divine Office.

Revised Version—a translation of the Bible into English made for the Protestant churches by scholars in England and America between 1870 and 1884, intended to correct some of the textual errors of the King James Version made in 1611.

Rubric (Lat. *ruber,* red)—directions printed in the liturgical books (Breviary, Missal, Ritual, etc.) in red letters to distinguish them from the text printed in black.

Sanhedrin—a Greek word signifying an assembly of judges, and adopted by the Hebrews to designate the Great Council of the temple under the presidency of the High Priest.

Sapiential Books—those of the seventy-two books contained in the Canon of the Catholic Bible that were neither legal, historical nor prophetic, but consist of reflections intended to teach wisdom. They are Job, Psalms, Proverbs, Ecclesiastes; Canticle of Canticles, Wisdom, and Ecclesiasticus.

Scriptoria—monastic institutions set apart for the copying of manuscripts before the art of printing created new facilities for making books.

Sedulius, Cælius—priest-poet of the fifth century, whose Latin verses descriptive of the life of Christ, His Blessed Mother and the details of sacred history have been incorporated in the liturgy of the Church.

Septuagint—a Greek version of the Bible also known as

Alexandrine Text, made at the instigation of King Ptolemy (III cent. B.C.) and adopted by the Jews of the dispersed tribes who had lost the use of the Hebrew tongue.

Sext—name of one of the Little Hours.

Sinaitic Text—a Greek MS. of the Bible made in the fourth or fifth century of Christ and discovered in the convent of St. Catherine on Mount Sinai.

Sophia—a Greek word meaning wisdom, and used to designate the Book of Wisdom in the Bible.

Talmud—a Jewish commentary on the Pentateuch, constituting a collection of civil and religious ordinances and traditions taught in the Rabbinical schools.

Terce—name of one of the Little Hours.

Thora (Hebrew for Law)—comprising the Law of Moses, or the Pentateuch. In a wider sense, used for the Hebrew Bible as a whole.

Totum (Lat. "the whole.")—A term designating a volume in which all the canonical Offices of the year are contained; otherwise they are separated so as to correspond to the four seasons, called Pars Verna, Pars Æstiva, Pars Autumnalis and Pars Hiemalis.

Vatican Council—the last General Council of the Catholic Church (twentieth) convoked by Pius IX in 1869, and interrupted by the Franco-Prussian War, 1870. It defined a number of dogmatic constitutions among which the infallibility of the Supreme Pontiff in matters of faith and morals when speaking *ex cathedra;* that is, officially as the interpreter of Christian doctrine. Disciplinary and reformatory acts, among which is the revision of the Roman Breviary, remained uncompleted and may be resumed at an early date.

Vatican Text—a Greek MS. of the Bible made in the

fourth century and preserved in the Vatican Library, at Rome.

Vespers—the official evening prayer of the Church, as found in the canonical Office of the Breviary. It consists of psalms, hymns and prayers adapted to the ecclesiastical season and the feasts throughout the year.

INDEX

A solis ortus cardine 165
Abecedarian Ode, the 167
Acts of the Apostles 13
Advent 57, 66, 67, 119, 166
Alma Redemptoris Mater, author of 57
Ambrose, St., hymn of 174
antiphon, intoning, 104
  origin of 105
antiphonaries, origin of 97
Aperi Domine 84
Apocalypse 13
Audite coeli, quæ loquor. 157
Authority, spiritual and secular 19
Balm of Gilead, symbolism of 61
Balsam, symbolism of 61
Beatus vir 141
Benedict, St., and chanting of the office 96
Benedictus
  of David 160
  of Zachary 162
Benedictus es, Domine 160
Bernard of Clairvaux, St., and Salve Regina 58
Bible 12
  a commentary on the Bible 12
  a thesaurus of 14
  and public worship 12
  and the "vicious circle" 19
  Catholics and 10-12
  didactic books of 34

AUTOBIOGRAPHY OF AN OLD BREVIARY

Bishop
  authority of 21
Breviary
  a commentary on the Bible 23
  early history of 93
  Gregorian calendar 128
  Leo X and 111
  Pius V 110
  reform of 109
  reverent recitation 83, 88
  St. Jerome 123
  Vatican Council and, 128
Breviary
  of Cardinal Quiñones 110
Breviary, the
  a commentary on the Bible 12
Caesar, Julius, and the calendar 70
calendar
  reform of 72, 113
  reform of, 70
Cantemus Domino 156
Canticles 156
Cedar, the, symbolism of 55
Chaplets of prayer, origin of 97
Christ
  Divinity of 22
Christ
  life of, in cycle of Church 119
Christmas 66, 67
Christmastide 13
Church
  infallibility 20

INDEX

under the apostles 93
Commission on Reform of the Breviary 111
Confitebor tibi Domine 158
Confitemini Domino 158
Creator alme siderum 166
Cross of the Scriptures, the 33
"Crudelis Herodes, Deum" 165
Cycle, lunar 73
Cypress, the, symbolism of 140
Damasus, St., and the Office 124
Daniel 30
"Dark Ages" 17
David 160
Directorium, the 65
Divine Office
  chanting of 120
  lay recitation 97
  monastic recitation 96
  seven hours of 117
  St. Jerome 107
Dominical Letter 73
Duplex feasts 104
Easter 13, 66
  how to reckon 73, 76
  origin of 129
Ecclesiastes, and Ecclesiasticus 14
Ecclesiasticus, canticle of 162
Elizabeth of Portugal, St. hymn in honor of 176
Epact 73
Epiphany 66
  and Invitatory 105

Epistles of Mass 12
Ezechias, Canticle of 161
Ezechiel 55
Fathers of the Church, hymns of 174
Feasts
  movable 68
Fortunatus, St., hymn of 171
Four, symbolism of 118
Gallican 96, 107, 114, 124
Gallican psalter 95
  and the Antiphonary of Bangor 96
Genesis, stories from 122
Golden Alphabet 145
Golden Number 73
Gospels, historical documents 20
Gospels, of Mass 12
government
  government of 21
Greek translations of the Bible 28
Gregory XIII and the calendar 72
Gregory, St., hymn of 174
Habacuc, lament of 161
Hallel Psalms 103, 146
Hannah, chant of 163
Hebrew Bible 29
Hermann Contractus 57
Hilary of Poitier, St., hymn of 175
Hymns of the Breviary 175
Inquisition, the 16
inspiration of the Breviary 122
Introid of the Mass in the early Church 94
Introit of the Mass in the early Church 95

INDEX

Invitatory, the 101
Ireland, early monastic schools in 34
Isaias
  canticle of 158
  prophecies of 55
Iste confessor 177
Itala Latin 47, 107, 112
Jeremias 13
  Canticle of 159
Jerome 95
Jerome, St. and the Septuagint 47
Jerome, St. Vulgate of 114
Jerome, St., revises the Breviary 107
Jesu Redemptor omnium 167
Jesus Ben Sirach 161
Jube, Domine, benedicere 96
Judith, canticle of 161
Kings, books of 14
Law and the priest 25
lawyers, American and English 24
Leap Year 70, 73
Lent 13, 67
Leo X and the breviary 111
Lessons
  from Genesis 122
  of the Second Nocturn 126
Lily, symbolism of 62
Little Offices, origin of 97
Liturgy, development of 112
Luther and the Palestinian version 28
Magnificat, the 163
Martina, St., hymn in honor of 175

Mary, Blessed Virgin
  in the New Testament 53
  symbols of 52
Mass
  and the Pasch 147
  Epistles and Gospels of 12
  in the early Church 94
  Introit of 94
Mass
  the secret of 94
Matins, order of 120
Meditation on the Office 46
Meton 73
Mizmor 7, 132
"Moral intention" explained 25
Moses
  Books of 13
  First Canticle of 156
  Second Canticle of 157
Myrrh
  symbolism of 60
Nard
  symbolism of 60
Neale, Dr. J.M. 168
Nunc dimittis 163
Nuns, Catholic 18
Officium de B. Maria V. 52
Olive, symbolism of 52
ordinandi, examination of 134
Ordinary of the Breviary, the 101
Ordo, the 66
Palestinian Bible, the 28

INDEX

palm tree, symbolism of 53
Paschal celebration, rite of 147
Passiontide 13
Paul, St., Epistles of 13
Pentecost 13, 44, 66, 93, 175
philanthropy, Catholic and Protestant 17
Pius V and the Breviary 81, 110
Prayers, repetition of 105, 128
Prophets, minor 14
Proverbs 14
Prudentius, hymn by 172
Psalm
  118 (119 Revised Version) 27
Psalm
  94 102
Psalms, grouping 133
Psalter 13
  contents of 132
  Irish 33
Quiñones, Cardinal, Breviary of 110
Rabanus Maurus, hymn of 177
Revised Version, divergences of 27
Russians, the, and the Gregorian calendar 72
Salve Regina, history of 56
Sapientiæ Liber 47
Second Nocturn, the 108, 120
Sedulius 165, 167-169, 171
Septuagesima 13
Septuagint
  and St. Jerome's translation 115
Septuagint version 28, 116

AUTOBIOGRAPHY OF AN OLD BREVIARY

Seven Hours 117
Seven, symbolism of 117
Simeon, Canticle of 162
Solomon and the Book of Wisdom 47
Temporal power of the Church 21
Theresa, St., hymn in honor of 177
Thora, the 28, 162
three, symbolism 117
Tobias, canticle of 161
Totum, the birth of 7
Trium Puerorum, Cantica 159
Tytinillus 85
Urban VIII, correctors 165, 167
Vatican Council and the Breviary 128
Venite exultemus 102, 123
Verbum supernum prodiens 166
Verses and Responses, origin of 105
Vespers, beginning of the Office 120
Vexilla Regis 178
"Vicious circle" and the Bible 19
Vowels of the Hebrew text 29
Wolverad, Hermann 57
Worship, liturgical, origin of 93
Zachary, Canticle of 162

www.ingramcontent.com/pod-product-compliance
Lightning Source LLC
Chambersburg PA
CBHW021442070526
44577CB00002B/251